Wales' Central Organising Principle

Legislating for Sustainable Development

Edited by
Anna Nicholl and John Osmond

In association with:

WWF Cymru

Cynnal Cymru/Sustain Wales

The Institute of Welsh Affairs exists to promote quality research and informed debate affecting the cultural, social, political and economic well being of Wales. The IWA is an independent organisation owing no allegiance to any political or economic interest group. Our only interest is in seeing Wales flourish as a country in which to work and live. We are funded by a range of organisations and individuals, including the Joseph Rowntree Charitable Trust, the Esmée Fairbairn Foundation, the Waterloo Foundation and PricewaterhouseCoopers. For more information about the Institute, its publications, and how to join, either as an individual or corporate supporter, contact:

IWA - Institute of Welsh Affairs
4 Cathedral Road, Cardiff CF11 9LJ

tel: 029 2066 0820
fax: 029 2023 3741
email: wales@iwa.org.uk
www.iwa.org.uk
www.clickonwales.org

ISBN: 978 1 904773 62 7

iwa

Contents

Introduction
Anna Nicholl

In line with the Labour Party's manifesto commitment at the 2011 Assembly election, the present Welsh Government has committed to legislate to make sustainable development its central organising principle. This will be the first piece of primary legislation dedicated to sustainable development in the United Kingdom and has the potential to be a world leader. An initial discussion document was issued for consultation in early 2012. A further consultation document appeared in May ahead of a White Paper in the autumn. The draft Bill will be introduced in the autumn of 2013.

In an effort to engage with this policy process, the Institute of Welsh Affairs teamed up with partners to arrange a series of events. The first was a conference held at University of Wales, Trinity Saint David in January 2012, organised jointly with Wales' Commissioner for Sustainable Futures, Peter Davies, WWF Cymru, Cynnal Cymru/ Sustain Wales, the Wales Centre for International Affairs, and the Institute for Sustainable Practice, Innovation and Resource Effectiveness at Trinity St David. The conference attracted over 100 delegates and some lively debate. This publication presents a series of papers based on the contributions made by speakers at the event.

Together the papers explain why legislation to embed sustainable development as a 'central organising principle' of government needs to be more than a paper exercise. If we continue with our current model of development, we face serious social, economic and environmental difficulties in the medium to long term, as the contributions from Gareth Wyn Jones and Anne Meikle demonstrate. We have already exceeded the earth's limits on a number of indicators and it looks increasingly difficult to halt climate change from breaching the +2°C limit. The prognosis is bleak in terms of reaching environmental limits. Stephen Palmer's paper demonstrates this is equally true for social policy as well.

We remain far away from achieving sustainable development whether in Wales, the UK, Europe or the rest of the world. In her contribution Andrea Ross reminds us that, whilst we can be proud of having indicators in Wales, they actually demonstrate that on many important counts, things are getting worse. Of course, all of this is happening in the wake of a global economic downturn, a relatively weak Welsh economy and deep cuts to public spending which will have serious social impacts.

There is no disagreement from contributors on the need for action across all areas of society. Jane Davidson, Andy Middleton and Gareth Wyn Jones emphasise the need to be bold in our thinking, setting out new ways of doing things rather than tinkering with the current system. This is not something that can be achieved through legislation alone. However, government does have an important part to play. As Susan Baker and Katarina Eckerberg argue in their contribution, there is need for agreement on strong and focussed legislation.

Most importantly, the legislation needs to be effective. This will mean striking a difficult balance between clarity and flexibility. The Bill needs to give government, business and civil society clear directions, but in a way that brings partners to the table, builds commitment and stimulates innovation. Several of the contributors call for the legislation to be easy to understand. Tim Peppin gives the strongest clarion call for it to be non-bureaucratic, with processes that are open and transparent so that decision-makers can be held to account. He also asks whether the Bill should be repealing legislation that hinders sustainable development, in addition to providing new tools.

There's an expectation amongst the contributors that the legislation should provide a clearer process for decision-making. Whilst this must be one of the objectives, the legislation cannot realistically provide a neat formula to resolve all the difficult decisions. Neither can it water down the complex reality of competing priorities or the different views on what is the most sustainable form of development in specific situations.

Shifting to a sustainable model of development is a global challenge. Several contributors refer to the importance of the Rio+20 Earth Summit in June 2012 and the hopes and fears around achieving much needed agreements. The Bill must work within the UK and European contexts as well as providing the framework for local government to deliver.

However, the contributors argue persuasively that Wales cannot wait for global agreements. We must continue to push at the boundaries and create the best framework for sustainable development within Wales. Indeed, given the Welsh Government's commitment to a strong governance model for sustainable development, Wales should have much to contribute to discussions on developing appropriate institutional frameworks at Rio+20.

The papers provide international comparisons to support discussion on appropriate models for Wales. Sándor Fülöp sets out his experience as Hungarian Ombudsman for Future Generations and the lessons he learned. He also draws on other international models of Commissioners and Ombudsmen. Peter Davies refers to his research of previous proposals for an independent Commission on sustainable development in Australia. Susan Baker and Katarina Eckerberg provide comparisons between governance models used across Europe.

Most of the discussion in this volume is concerned with the content of the forthcoming Welsh Sustainable Development Bill. A key issue is whether a definition should be set out and if so, what might it be. Peter Roderick, Jane Davidson, Andrea Ross, and Anne Meikle argue strongly for clarifying the definition. Ambiguity has proved problematic in the past. There is discussion as to whether this might best be done on the face of the Bill or via a statutory strategy.

The discussions on definitions demonstrate that there are still many different interpretations of what we mean by 'sustainable development'. Some argue that the Bill must continue to make clear that is has economic and social as well as environmental dimensions. On the other hand, Andrea Ross argues that this has been one of the main causes of confusion, leading to an impossible attempt to balance the three, which the Bill should now resolve. For Ross, "sustainable development needs to be redefined in a meaningful way, with clear limits and priorities that focus on ecological sustainability and wellbeing instead of economic growth."

Perhaps there isn't as much conflict as initially appears. Several contributions, particularly those from Peter Roderick, Anne Meikle and Gareth Wyn Jones, leave us in no doubt that as a society we need to change to ensure we live within the Earth's limits. If we do not we will face serious social and economic problems. Meikle argues that, set out by the Welsh Government in 2009, sustainable development should be, "clear that it retains a commitment to living within environmental limits", as well as leaving "no room for doubt that sustainable development is about social, economic and environmental well-being".

Gareth Wyn Jones' contribution sets out in detailed and stark terms the scale of the challenge we face in the coming decades, plus the consequences of a failure to adapt. An earlier version of his paper was tabled ahead of the conference and has framed much of our discussion and debate. At the end of his paper he sets out the beginnings of an approach that would put our economy and society on a more constructive course. His quotation from Raymond Williams is particularly apt in this regard: "... to be truly radical is to make hope possible rather than despair convincing."

Can the Bill help us move beyond the conflict of environment versus economy within our current system? Can we develop, as Gareth Wyn Jones urges, a new paradigm for economic development that operates within ecological limitations?

Stephen Palmer reminds us that sustainable development's focus on the well being of future generations is just as applicable within social policy as it is in environmental policy and is just as urgent. As outlined in the Welsh Government's discussion document, sustainable development emphasises the longer term, as well as better integration across social, economic and environmental policy areas.

Contributors discuss what duty the Bill might place on Ministers and public bodies in order to achieve sustainable development as the Welsh Government's 'central organising principle'. In particular, Peter Roderick and Andrea Ross argue that a clear and strong a duty must be placed on Ministers. In the conference lawyer Emyr Lewis drew on his experience of the Children's Rights and Welsh Language Measure to caution on the different implications of sustainable development in the 'decision-making process' rather than in the 'exercise of functions'. Simply having a 'due regard' can get in the way of a 'duty' to exercise functions to achieve sustainable development. Effective legislation will need to lay down meaningful consequences if it is contravened.

Many of the contributors discuss the potential role of the Commissioner and present different models for the way she or he might operate. There is agreement that the Commissioner will need to have teeth and be properly independent.

Many contributors also raise the importance of strong participation and engagement in developing policy and in delivering sustainable development. Civil society must be involved but it is equally important to engage the business community and social partners. In the conference Baroness Eluned Morgan, SWALEC's Director of Low Carbon Business Development, was keen to emphasise that many businesses are leading the way on sustainable development in finding low alternatives in their production processes. It's important that they are proactively engaged. Participation is something that needs to be set out in the Bill.

Many contributors also call for the Bill to introduce a statutory sustainable development strategy that would flesh out what government and other public bodies must do in order to make a reality of sustainable development as the central organising principle. Peter Davies examines whether this might be a role for the Commissioner. Anne Meikle and Peter Roderick also argue for the precautionary principle and for decisions to be based on sound science to be included within the Bill. They also press for the inclusion of a Welsh Charter of Environmental Rights which would guarantee the right to live in a healthy environment. This would be enforceable in the Welsh courts in the same way as human rights are enforceable under the Human Rights Act.

Our hope is that this publication will help stimulate further thinking along these lines, and support wider engagement in the debates over the coming months as the Sustainable Development Bill is drafted and makes its way through the National Assembly.

Chapter 1
Taking the longer view
Peter Roderick

Our values lead us to support the development of a more equal society, in which every Welsh citizen is able to make the most of their abilities and contribute to the wider community in which they live. We seek to improve the well being of all. We also recognize our responsibility to future generations and will continue to build a more sustainable Wales.
Welsh Labour Party Manifesto, 2011

Human activities have developed to a point where our actions impact not just on other people and our local environment, but the whole planet and the conditions of life for centuries to come. We are now facing serious and threatening environmental problems as never before.[1] Our responsibility to future generations has been recognised by the previous Welsh Government. But progress has been patchy, and much still remains to be done.

The National Assembly now has new primary law-making powers. An Assembly Act cannot impose duties, confer powers or otherwise apply in relation to any subject not listed in Schedule 7, Part 1 of the Government of Wales Act 2006. Neither can it modify section 79 of that Act under which Welsh Ministers must make a scheme on how they propose to promote sustainable development. However, these limitations, do not prevent a comprehensive and coherent legislative package from being enacted, aimed at providing a long-term framework to help safeguard the future.

This can be achieved by an Act of the Assembly firstly by requiring Welsh Ministers to exercise their duties and powers in order to achieve sustainable development, to adopt a sustainable development strategy, to make sustainable development the central organising principle of government and by enacting the precautionary principle.

Secondly, an Act should acknowledge the existence of environmental limits, and Wales' need to keep within them, by starting to establish a system respecting planetary boundaries which would evolve over time. A third limb of the Act should put the Commissioner for Sustainable Futures on a statutory footing as a strong and independent champion of the environment and future generations, with significant powers and duties.

The Act should also establish a bold and inspiring Welsh Charter of Environmental Rights, which would help to raise awareness beyond policy makers of the predicament we now face and to prevent and remedy environmental injustice, suffered disproportionately by poorer people.

Each of these areas is summarised briefly as follows:

Sustainable development

An Act should go beyond the current duty in section 79 by requiring Welsh Ministers to exercise their (other) duties and powers in order to achieve sustainable development. This strengthened duty should be supplemented by a legally-required sustainable development strategy which would become the main mechanism for achieving sustainable development. The strategy should be given specific legal consequences, such as requiring specified public bodies to frame their sustainable development objectives by reference to it. In this way it and would become the lynchpin for making sustainable development the central organising principle of government. It would set out the processes that would ensure that the Welsh Government's sustainable development policies are coordinated, consistent and coherent, including processes for the resolution of conflicting priorities.

The strategy would be presented to the Assembly by the First Minister, and monitored and audited independently. It would be possible to require the Assembly's approval of the strategy before it became formally adopted, as well as the Assembly being given powers to require reviews. The Act should also define sustainable development, and require the precautionary principle to be applied by Ministers in the exercise of their duties and powers.

Environmental limits

An Act should acknowledge environmental limits by starting to establish a statutory system to recognise the biophysical preconditions necessary for human development in line with the planetary boundaries concept. The system would begin by setting out a process to establish in law those Earth-system processes that are necessary for the resilience of the Earth and of the natural environment of Wales. It would evolve over time and relate to the ecosystem approach. Local and public authorities would also be covered, whilst recognising the need for action at the UK, EU and international levels as well, such as at the 2012 meeting in Rio de Janeiro to mark twenty years since the UN Conference on Environment and Development.

Commissioner for Sustainable Futures

The Commissioner for Sustainable Futures should be put on a statutory footing as a strong champion of the environment and future generations elected by and accountable to Assembly Members, and independent of the executive and legislature. The Commissioner would have the duty of investigating complaints from members of the public, or on his or her own volition. This duty would be backed up by the power to request other public bodies, such as the Environment Agency, to use its powers to prevent actual or potential environmental damage.

In cases of inaction the Commissioner should be empowered to seek the intervention of the courts to counter the threat of serious environmental harm. This investigative duty would be aimed at holding the government and other public authorities to account, and preventing environmental degradation. The Commissioner would also have research, advice and reporting roles, including in relation to the strengthened sustainable development duty and planetary boundaries.

In this way, the Commissioner would not only be a spokesperson for present and future generations of people in Wales, but would have real powers. This would demonstrate that policy delivery is as important as policy formulation not only as a matter of intent, but in actual fact. Locating such a position within the Welsh Government, or even within the Assembly, would not give him or her much credibility outside 'the Bay'. It would not encourage the Commissioner to exercise his or her functions without fear of prejudice or hope of advantage. Locating it outside the Bay would be a waste of time and money if no real powers were to be enacted.

Environmental rights

An Act should establish a Welsh Charter of Environmental Rights, guaranteeing the right to live in a healthy environment which would be enforceable in the Welsh courts in the same way as human rights are enforceable under the Human Rights Act. The right has been acknowledged in many constitutions around the world. The Council of Europe's Parliamentary Assembly has recommended its addition to the European Convention on Human Rights, and the UK has acknowledged it in ratifying the Århus Convention. This would be a bold and inspiring step for the Assembly to take, motivated by its long-term vision for Wales. It would help to raise awareness beyond policy makers of the predicament we now face; and by guaranteeing rights that would be enforceable against politicians and public authorities it would help to prevent and remedy environmental injustice, suffered disproportionately by poorer people.

Notes

1   WWF Cymru commissioned Peter Roderick to provide a discussion document setting out legislative options for the National Assembly for Wales. This was published on its website in June 2011 and formed the basis of Peter Roderick's contribution to the January 2012 conference. The full version of the paper can be found at: http://assets.wwf.org.uk/downloads/dicsussion_document_by_peter_roderick_the_national_assembly_for_wales_and_taking_th.pdf. Related discussion papers can also be found at wales.wwf.org.uk/government.

Chapter 2
The global imperative
Anne Meikle

It is 20 years since the first Earth Summit in Rio produced international agreements to deliver sustainable development. This was when the global community, Governments, local authorities, trade unions and voluntary bodies came to an unprecedented global agreement to seek better ways for people to live. It sought to ensure there would be enough resources for us all, and that people lived fairer lives through eradicating poverty and decreasing disparities in standards of living.

These were key ideas that started to change the way the world operates and is organised. So eradicating poverty, increasing equity and safeguarding the environment were key areas for attention. I would also argue that it set Wales on the course which now, 20 years later in the year of another Earth Summit, has led to the Welsh Government intending to enshrine those principles in law, through a Sustainable Development Bill.

Sustainable development is *not* just about the environment. It is also about the integrated delivery of social, economic and environmental objectives. Therefore, it's about the sustainable use of resources, equity, and wellbeing. Without healthy, functioning ecosystems and other biophysical processes, we cannot have healthy, prosperous lives. As the Sustainable Development Commission made clear in its 2006 report *I will if You will*, "living within ecological limits is the non-negotiable basis for our social and economic development". Accordingly, one of the prime functions of the Welsh Sustainable Development Bill must be to ensure that we take a global perspective on developing an environmentally sustainable future.

Wales was one of the first industrialised countries and has historically pumped out large quantities of greenhouse gases, and we continue to do so. At the 1992 Rio Earth summit the UK signed up to the following principle:

> "The developed countries acknowledge the responsibility that they bear in the international pursuit of sustainable development in view of the pressures their societies place on the global environment and of the technologies and financial resources they command."

In Wales we are divorced from many of the environmental consequences of our lifestyles. Unlike those in many developing countries we don't chop down trees for firewood or to make space for oil palm plantations. So it can be hard for us to recognise the global impact of how we live and work. It is also easy for us to forget that our economy depends on natural resources and a stable climate. As a result the value of the services nature provides is frequently underestimated or ignored in decision-making.

Policies that promote a shift away from fossil fuels will reduce the Welsh economy's exposure to volatile energy prices and climate change impacts. We can address current economic challenges by building a greener economy with secure jobs, clean energy and protection for our natural environment.

Humanity faces a profound dilemma. On the one hand, economic growth is central to the functioning of the current economic system. Employment, company profits, and government revenue for public services are all dependent on growth. Yet the kind of economic growth we now have is unsustainable. It depends on energy from fossil fuels that threatens climate stability. It also damages the natural systems that provide the conditions for life that enable humans and nature to thrive. In its submission to this year's Earth summit the EU Council declared:

> "The world is facing multiple crises and challenges that are mutually interlinked. In this broader context Rio+20 provides a unique opportunity to rethink the current perception of growth and consumption, inclusion and how we utilize our limited resources, thereby safeguarding the needs of future generations."[1]

Our ability to live on this planet depends on ecosystems functioning healthily. However, the resilience of our environment is being increasingly challenged by our over-exploitation of our natural resources and the consequences of climate change. Demand continues to grow and resources are becoming increasingly scarce. Such scarcity is not only an environmental problem. It bears directly on our economy and society. For example, analysts suggest we have already passed peak oil production, are approaching peak gas, while peak lithium and phosphorus production are on the horizon.

Poor people are the most vulnerable to resource scarcity and environmental shocks, as we can already see in Wales with increasing numbers falling into fuel poverty. On a global scale, by 2007 we were already using 1.5 planet's worth of resources (as measured by ecological footprint). However, the situation in Wales is worse. If everyone lived the way we do then we would need nearly 2.5 planets. In the long term the world cannot provide sufficient resources for everyone to live like this. Therefore, as developing countries become more affluent and aspire to our lifestyles, there is an impossible conundrum.

This was recognised as far back as the 1987, in the Brundtland Report, *Our Common Future*, which stated that:

> "...physical sustainability cannot be secured unless development policies pay attention to such considerations as changes in *access to resources* and in the *distribution of costs and benefits*... physical sustainability implies a concern for social equity between generations, a concern that must logically be extended to equity within each generation."[2]

The prominence of these concerns explains the major role played in the Rio Earth Summit by trade unions as well as international development non-government organisations. This has prompted ethical concerns about manufacturing. Are your shoes or carpets produced by child or slave labour? That's as much a sustainable development issue as the pollution and overfishing of our oceans.

As Mahatma Ghandi said, "Earth provides enough for every man's needs but not enough for every man's greed". To ensure access to a reasonable standard of living for all, we need to consider a fairer access to resources. This is the aspiration that WWF enshrined in the idea of a *One Planet Wales*, for the people of Wales to lead happy, healthy, prosperous lives within their fair share of the earth's resources.[3]

The Government recognises this and explicitly sets out in its policy document *One Wales One Planet* to ensure that Wales lives within in its *fair* share of the earth's resources. Environmental sustainability and social justice are interdependent. Issues such as fuel poverty, flood insurance, access to services and jobs are all related to managing our environment and resources sustainably.

The transition to a low carbon, resource efficient *One Planet* economy is therefore crucial for business, for jobs, for people and the environment. Supporting this transition is a vital role for the Welsh Government, local authorities and businesses. How can legislation contribute to achieving this?

The Welsh Government should take this opportunity to *strengthen its duty to sustainable development* and to define this clearly, according to the *One Wales, One Planet* definition. This would include explicit recognition of 'living within environmental limits' and enshrining respect for planetary boundaries. To be truly inspiring the legislation would enshrine a Welsh charter of environmental rights in law. In this way the National Assembly would guarantee our right to live in a healthy environment.

If the Act is passed through the Assembly with cross party support then we will be providing certainty for the future. Businesses and others could be reasonably sure that this was a long-term commitment and would be pursued regardless of the political make up of government. That is what investors always ask for and should be a valuable selling point for the Welsh economy. After all, sustainable development is about long-term change and so needs long-term, consistent commitment. Such certainty and continuity through the political cycles can be achieved if there continues to be cross-party support.

In 2011 an Ipsos Mori survey found that 72 per cent of Welsh adults agreed that sustainable development should play a central part in decision-making in Wales. All Welsh political parties should be emboldened by this support. The legislation *should* change the culture of the public sector and its decision-making processes. It must affect how our money is spent and lead to different outcomes. If it does not then it will be a waste of legislative time and energy.

The legislation should change the way decisions are made so they are considerate of future generations, global impacts and local communities. With a stronger sustainable development duty, we would expect to minimise future negative impacts and inherited liabilities for future decision makers. For example, planning permissions on flood plains increase the liabilities on local authorities, the Environment Agency and possibly the developers for increased flood defence costs, as climate change affects the severity of storms and rainfall. They can also increase insurance costs for homeowners and occupiers. Such long term costs and liabilities should be factored into decisions.

If it is accompanied by good statutory guidance and a Commissioner with real independence and powers, the legislation will change outcomes. There needs to be a paradigm shift in public service delivery and leadership from all politicians to ensure the public understand and support the changes, even though there will be hard choices ahead.

Some good examples of long-term thinking are already in place in health and education. For example, more resources are going into preventing ill health through, improved diet, and in improving education outcomes by focusing on early years provision. However, isolated good practice will not change the nature of Wales and its society.

Time to deliver

There is widespread recognition that our present practices are damaging the environment. Moreover, there is widespread agreement about the urgency of tackling climate change and the costs of delay.[4] We know that the current economic system is crumbling fiscally, and that the world's resources must be shared more equitably to prevent drastic consequences for the disadvantaged from rising prices, water shortages and impacts of climate change. We know, too, that bold leadership and foresight are required rather than incrementalism. Why then have we not acted?

The recent independent review of Welsh Government performance on embedding sustainable development across government drew the same conclusion as WWF Cymru drew in 2011 and that the Wales Audit Office drew in 2010.[5] It was that the Welsh Government is making good progress in many departments and policy areas but it is not consistent. Officials are still not clear what sustainable development means and there is no clear plan for delivery. It is very likely that this is the case across much of the public sector, despite 20 years having passed since the first local authority signed up to Agenda 21.

A Sustainable Development Act can make delivery a priority for everyone in the public sector. To be effective it will have to specify what this means, through a clear definition of sustainable development and of how this can be made the Welsh Government's 'central organising principle'.

To be truly effective there must be consequences for non-compliance with public bodies made open to challenge. It is vital that Wales Audit office, Assembly Committees and new governance structures at local authority level consider the interests of future generations in their scrutiny.

Strengthening the duty

To achieve this we must strengthen the current duty by requiring Welsh Ministers to exercise their functions in order to *achieve* sustainable development. At the moment, Ministers need only write down how they propose to promote sustainable development. There is no requirement to actually deliver it.

We have been fortunate that successive governments have taken the sustainable development obligation in current legislation – the 1999 and 2006 Wales Acts - fairly seriously and gone further than legally required. However, the reviews show this is not consistently the case. If the Assembly strengthens the duty as we suggest, hopefully with cross party consensus, then there should be more consistency across government. There should also be more certainty for civil servants, businesses and others as to the long-term intentions of all future Welsh Governments.

The duty should apply to all decisions, including budgetary proposals. This is critical. Much of the influence that Government and the public sector have is through their large expenditure on goods and services. As we have seen with pilot projects, like *Arbed* in the housing sector, sustainable procurement can increase local skills and job opportunities as well as cutting heating bills. Such procurement financial matters must be included in the Bill.

If we are to achieve the kind of change in the economy that international experts within the United Nations and European Union experts tell us is necessary, then we must have consistent efforts from the public sector to lever change in the private sector. The EU Council states there must be "concrete efforts to promote sustainable procurement as a core element in creating a green economy".

This strengthened duty should be supplemented by a legally required sustainable development strategy that would become the main mechanism for implementation. The strategy should be given specific legal consequences, such as requiring specified public bodies to frame their sustainable development objectives by reference to it. It would become the lynchpin for making sustainable development the central organising principle of government by setting out the processes that would ensure that policies in relation to sustainable development are coordinated, consistent and coherent, including processes for the resolution of conflicting priorities.

There must be *statutory* guidance to other public bodies. The public sector must think about the long term as well as the here and now. Such guidance, accompanied by targets and performance indicators can encourage a shift in the culture towards one of legacy as well as service delivery.

It *must* be clear that sustainable development is the overarching priority, not one of a number of competing priorities. The latest review on Government performance recommended a better alignment between the programme for government and the Sustainable Development scheme. Back in 2006, a Whitehall report reviewing statutory duties on sustainable development, noted that, "strategies were undermined by the proliferation of strategies with lack of clarity over which strategy took precedence."[6]

Definition

The Act should make it clear what sustainable development means. This must leave no room for doubt that sustainable development is about social, economic and environmental wellbeing. However, we believe it must be very clear that it retains commitment to living within environmental limits.

The current definition was established in 2009 and effectively recognises environmental limits and social justice issues, partly through the concept of 'living within a fair share of Earth's resources'. It currently states:

> "In Wales, sustainable development means enhancing the economic, social and environmental wellbeing of people and communities, achieving a better quality of life for our own and future generations:
>
> - in ways which promote social justice and equality of opportunity; and
> - in ways which enhance the natural and cultural environment and respect its limits - using only our fair share of the earth's resources and sustaining our cultural legacy. Sustainable development is the process by which we reach the goal of sustainability."

Environmental limits

However, this may be the time to look at the latest thinking on planetary boundaries. In 2009 29 scientists wrote in the magazine *Nature*:

> "We have tried to identify the Earth-system processes and associated thresholds which, if crossed, could generate unacceptable environmental change. Nine such processes have been identified, which are critical to our ability to live on Earth and, for which it is necessary to define planetary boundaries: climate change; rate of biodiversity loss (terrestrial and marine); interference with the nitrogen and phosphorous cycles; stratospheric ozone depletion; ocean acidification; global freshwater use; change in land use; chemical pollution; and atmospheric aerosol loading... Analysis suggests that three of the earth-system processes - climate change, rate of biodiversity loss and interference with the nitrogen cycle -

have already transgressed their boundaries."[7]

It would be wise for the Welsh Government to recognise these biophysical preconditions for human development in the legislation and establish a process for identifying how they can be respected. As the Brundtland report noted:

> "… ultimate limits there are, and sustainability requires that long before these are reached, the world must ensure equitable access to the constrained resource and reorient technological efforts."

The Act also needs to ensure compliance with other principles of sustainable development, as recognised by the UK government and others, which are currently contained in *One Wales One Planet* as overarching or supporting principles.

These include using sound science responsibly but also applying the precautionary principle, that is *"we will use an evidence-based approach to decision-making but, where there are threats of serious or irreversible damage, lack of full scientific certainty shall not be used as a reason for postponing cost-effective measures to prevent environmental degradation."* It is vital that this principle is given a statutory basis.

Legislation alone is not enough. It is essential that it is supported and scrutinised. In 2004, a report for the Office of the Deputy Prime Minister examined the critical factors for the successful implementation of sustainable development. It found that the, "single most important factor determining an organisation's approach to sustainable development was management leadership".[8] Commitment from the very top and the drive from senior management are what ensures effective delivery. It will be particularly important to focus on this in economic development, which is so crucial to the delivery of sustainable development.

The next most important factors were the mechanisms in place for scrutinising delivery and external stakeholder pressure. If effectively resourced, a strong independent Commissioner for Sustainable Futures can provide support and advice to Government. However, the primary role is protecting the public from non-compliance or a lack of implementation. The Commissioner must be able to scrutinise, have access to information and the courts and seek remedies and mitigation. It may prove particularly important that they can act on behalf of future generations, maintaining the long-term view and speaking up for those who will have to bear the consequences of our actions.

In a difficult period of transition, an independent and authoritative voice which can work with the other commissioners and ombudsmen to ensure the public sector and government is held to account will be vital. True independence would be secured if the Commissioner was appointed by the National Assembly rather than the Welsh Government.

Should we be given a right to live in a healthy environment? A truly ambitious Act would show leadership by protecting Welsh citizens from the sort of harm to their health and environment which they have suffered over the last 150 years. Many countries around the world, such as Hungary, already recognise such rights. They would be enforceable against politicians and public authorities and would help to remedy the environmental injustice, suffered disproportionately by poorer people. It is often prohibitively expensive in the UK to go to court to seek a remedy of this nature. Using a Commissioner would improve the access to justice for many disadvantaged people. Can we perhaps dream of environmental rights to sit alongside those in the Children's Act or the Equalities legislation?

Notes

1   Council of the European Union, Rio+20: *Pathways to a Sustainable Future - Council conclusions*, March 9, 2012.

2   The Report of the World Commission on Environment and Development, *Our Common Future*, June 1987.

3   Ravetz, J. Bond, S. Meikle, A., *One Planet Wales*, Surrey. WWF UK, 2007.

4   Stern, N., *Review Report on the Economics of Climate Change*, HM Treasury, 2006

5   PricewaterhouseCoopers, *Effectiveness Review of the Sustainable development Scheme*, January 2012.

6   Cousens. S, *Review of Statutory Sustainable Development Duties*, In house Policy Consultancy, 2006.

7   Rockström, J, *et al*, 'A safe operating space for humanity', *Nature* 461: 472-475, 2009.

8   Egan Review, *Skills for Sustainable Communities*, Office of the Deputy Prime Minister, 2004.

Chapter 3
Systemic change the only game in town
Jane Davidson

Why do we need to legislate? As the architect of the commitment, one thing I discovered during my time as Minister in the Welsh Government is that small incremental improvements year on year are utterly insufficient for the global and local sustainability challenges ahead. Systemic change is the only game in town. The development of the sustainable development duty offers organisations in Wales an appropriate government hook to review their practices and test whether they are responding appropriately to 21st Century needs.

At the University of Wales Trinity Saint David, the commitment to educate more sustainably was catalysed by the Higher Education Academy's Green Academy programme. This encouraged universities across the UK to institutionalise sustainability. Eight universities were successful in gaining entry to the programme following a UK wide competitive process. Serendipitously for Trinity Saint David, entry coincided with the decision to merge two institutions to create this new transformed university in west Wales with sustainability at the heart of its strategic vision. The commitment recognises that the world is changing and the skills we need must change accordingly. Sustainability is on the agenda of many employers and the creative, interdisciplinary systems thinking that it encourages also enhances students' employability. The University governors are committed to ensuring that our students will enhance their skills and employability through their university experience. In practice this is being demonstrated by our new, virtual Institute for Sustainable Practice, Innovation and Resource Effectiveness (INSPIRE).

The University of Wales Trinity Saint David has made some key commitments to take this agenda forward, both by embedding sustainability into every student's experience and developing new opportunities. A new strategic alliance with the Centre for Alternative Technology will enhance the University's sustainability offer, not least because of its seminal work on Zero Carbon Britain 2030.

In west Wales, we have been afforded an opportunity to create systemic change at the university level in a country creating systemic change at the Welsh level. If we take the analogy further, and you look at the earth as a single complex system, the 21st Century challenge is to maintain the optimal conditions for life at a time when it is being menaced by terrestrial events. Taking the systemic approach also enables us to look at how we can make the system more resilient by understanding the interaction and the effect of action in one part of the world on another.

In the Science Museum in London is *Science On a Sphere (SOS)*®, a room-sized, global display system that uses computers and video projectors to project planetary data onto a six foot diameter sphere, analogous to a giant animated globe. It was developed as an educational tool to help illustrate Earth System science to people of all ages. Animated images of atmospheric storms, climate change, and ocean temperature can be shown on the sphere, to explain what are sometimes complex environmental processes in a captivating way. Sphere-casting can be used to map the progress of a tsunami or any other process. Of course, the data overlaid on it does not have to just be environmental as a recent demonstration of the transmission of H1N1 (commonly known as bird-flu) showed.

Our role as stewards of the system will be under scrutiny at the Rio Earth Summit in June 2012. The good news is that countries across the world accept that worldwide action needs to take place on climate change and biodiversity. There's also acceptance that such action needs to be framed in the context of sustainable development and to accommodate developed and developing countries.

The bad news is there is much more rhetoric about working together to tackle the problem than there is delivery. Thousands of politician hours across the world are spent in making commitments. Thousands of official support hours are spent writing 'non-documents' in the hope that somehow the right turn of phrase, the right couching of a project could lead to global agreement on actions – and turn a 'non-document' into a declaration.

The trouble with this kind of process is that in order for sufficient action to take place UN members would need to come to these meetings thinking globally, and being prepared to act locally. They would need to offer themselves up to appropriate monitoring and evaluation of their efforts to create a whole that is larger than the sum of its parts. Further, they would need to be altruistic, principled and confident of the evidence. Finally, they would need to see their country as part of the world system and not as a territory whose boundaries need protection. And therein lies the rub.

The stakes at the Rio Earth Summit are high. For the last few years there has been a global tussle about the future of the Kyoto Protocol due to expire in 2012. This is an important debate. Some argue that without a second Kyoto commitment period, climate change action will fall apart. Others look to new arrangements and hail the commitment to a future legal agreement made in Durban. What is certainly true is that there should be no backtracking of world effort when the physical evidence of climate change is amassing daily. There is a danger that global leaders will not be thinking and acting globally, but thinking and acting locally and walk away without a global agreement.

Having attended the UN climate change conferences at Posnam, Copenhagen and Cancun, and participated in attempts to reconcile the irreconcilable, I am convinced that voluntary agreements are insufficient to tackle the issues humanity faces. Instead, collective action on the scale and pace we need requires legal underpinning. The Earth Summit in Rio is almost upon us. Two key themes will be debated– the institutional framework for sustainable development and the green economy. In relation to sustainable development, the website tells us:

> "The scope of a theme such as the 'institutional framework for sustainable development' is potentially vast, as sustainable development is a wide and all-encompassing concept. However, for the purposes of the Earth Summit, this includes monitoring and enforcement of global agreements on environment and sustainable development."

All this is very worthy, but, as the website points out, there is no agreed definition of sustainable development. How, therefore, could global agreements be monitored or enforced? The other key agenda at the Earth Summit is the 'Green Economy'. Once again, there is as yet no agreed definition of what constitutes a green economy, but according to the website:

> "One strand approaches the question through the analysis of market failure and the internationalisation of externalities. Another takes a systemic view of the economic structure and its impact on relevant aspects of sustainable development. A third focuses on social goals (jobs, for example) and examines ancillary policies needed to reconcile social goals with the other objectives of economic policy. Finally, a fourth strand focuses on the macroeconomic framework and development strategy with the goal of identifying dynamic pathways towards sustainable development."

Somehow, I know that although the sentiments are right, the language is not going to lead to a storming of the barricades. But the measures proposed are definitely worthwhile:

1. Getting prices right, including removing fossil fuel subsidies, valuing natural resources and imposing taxes on things that harm the environment (environmental

'bads'). This is to support sustainable consumption and incentivize business choices. It builds upon some of the earliest writings in environmental economics.

2. Public procurement policies to promote greening of business and markets.

3. Ecological tax reforms based mainly on the experience of European countries. The basic idea is that shifting the tax base away from 'good' factors of production such as labour to 'bad' factors such as pollution will allow for a double dividend - correcting environmental degradation while boosting employment.

4. Public investment in sustainable infrastructure (including public transport, renewable energy and the retrofitting of existing infrastructure and buildings for improved energy efficiency). This is to restore, maintain and, where possible, enhance the stock of natural capital. This has particular salience within the current recessionary context, given the need for public expenditure on stimulus packages.

5. Targeted public support for research and development on environmentally sound technologies. This is partly in order to compensate for private underinvestment in pre-commercial research and development; partly to stimulate investments in critical areas (such as renewable energy); and partly to offset the bias of current research and development towards dirty and hazardous technologies.

6. Strategic investment through public sector development outlays. These will require incentive programmes and partnerships, in order to lay the foundation of a self-sustaining process of socially and environmentally sustainable economic growth.

7. Social policies to reconcile social goals with existing or proposed economic policies.

However, since the Green Economy has no legal or even agreed policy meaning, how do we get countries to take action? Here in the UK, a government which declared that it intended to be the 'greenest government ever' is rapidly backtracking. Despite evidence from Sir Nicholas Stern and others that we should be investing now to save in the future, one of the reasons climate change has dropped down the agenda is the recession. It is as though somehow acting on climate change is a luxury for the good times and not our best defence in the bad. Meanwhile, the planet pays no regard to politics and carries on regardless. The current mantra, that we can't afford to take action that might put our economy at a disadvantage, may ride roughshod over existing protections such as those in the planning system. Why is the argument that the green economy presents the best opportunity for sustainable job creation in a time of rising unemployment falling on deaf ears?

Each UN global conference, whether on sustainable development, biodiversity or climate change, is attempting to find a way forward on these tricky issues on a worldwide basis. And their work is valuable. If we take a systemic approach, then continuing global dialogue around these issues is important – and increasingly important as each year passes. But, it is not the game changer it was thought to be at the first Earth Summit. This is because unless individual countries are prepared to negotiate on a UN wide basis from a position of thinking globally and being prepared to go back to their own country and act locally in the interests of wider humanity, the *de minimus* position might just be that the world averts wars through this dialogue. Yet it does not achieve the global understanding necessary to preserve our ecosystem. I'm always reminded of what Nazmul Chowdhury, Head of Project at Practical Action in Bangladesh, said in 2009:

> "Forget about making poverty history. Climate Change will make poverty permanent."

As we approach this year's Earth Summit, we find ourselves in an interesting situation. Science and logic tell us to act one way, while individual countries often take decisions that are driven by neither. I don't believe that we should give up hope. Instead we need to reframe the debate. If the world goes to Rio this year without a clear idea of what sustainable development means, let's define it in law. This debate needs to be framed in a way that garners support across the political spectrum. It should also be clear legally and reintroduce a values system to politics and decision-making. I believe that the way forward is for countries to reframe their political debate in the context of sustainable development. Sustainability is our best defence.

Access to natural resources has always been a cause of conflict and a weapon of war. John Beddington, when Government Chief Scientist, identified the perfect storm of food shortages, water scarcity, insecure energy and a growing population. Lester Brown, President of the Earth Policy Institute says:

> "The threats to our security now are climate change, population growth, falling water tables, soil erosion, collapsing fisheries etc. And we can't say we don't have the resources to save civilisation; we do. The question is how we use those resources."

In many areas the challenge of providing food, energy and water for a growing population can't be met without collaboration. But could discussions about the environment provide a less charged political entry point for collaboration? Can initiatives to preserve ecosystems across political borders go some way to establishing peaceful relations between otherwise rival communities – in their enlightened self-interest? If so, how? It still requires clear commitment and laws at the country level to make changes.

The journey between the Earth Summits from 1992 to 2012 has delivered some action but not enough. Global opportunities facilitated by modern technology are not galvanising us into sufficient action and our day-to-day existence is inexorably local. I believe we have to redefine the terms of this engagement. We are in the territory of Geddes and Schumacher. With many economies now flat or in decline, financial systems in crisis and the climate increasingly erratic, can we seize a 'back to the future' moment for the ideas promoted in Schumacher's 1973 seminal text *Small is Beautiful* that questioned the drive for relentless GDP expansion?

That's what I believe can be offered by a country like Wales taking sustainability seriously. In many ways, the journey in Wales reflects the global journey.

When the National Assembly came into being in 1999 it had a unique duty to make a scheme on how it proposed to promote sustainable development in the exercise of its functions. Progress on the scheme was reported annually to Members and any incoming administration was required to review its effectiveness. This was seen as an extremely innovative and exciting duty, representing a new kind of democracy. Members from all parties supported it. Assembly Members often mentioned the existence of the Duty positively.

But, as was the case elsewhere throughout the world, there was no clear definition of sustainable development. There was broad support for what is usually known as the 'Brundtland' definition, after Dr Gro Harlem Brundtland, the Director General of the World Health Organisation and chair of Our Common Futures, the World Commission on the Environment and Development. As she expressed it, sustainability entails:

> "...development that meets the needs of the present without compromising the ability of future generations to meet their own needs."

It includes two important concepts: the concept of need, and in particular the essential needs of the world's poor, to which overriding priority should be given; coupled with the idea of limitations imposed by the state of technology and social organization on the environment's ability to meet present and future need.

But how was this to become real? Wales looked to learn from others. At the Earth Summit in Johannesburg in 2002 we became a founding member of nrg4SD, a global network of regional governments promoting sustainable development. With members across the world this acts as a voice and representative of sub-national governments. It is the only international network on sustainable development matters with a worldwide presence and representing solely sub-national governments. It is an important tier of operation in terms of getting things done. As Jonathan Porritt, when Chair of the Sustainable Development Commission, said:

> "Wales and Scotland may well be close to the 'Goldilocks' (just right) scale for doing SD. A common refrain from policymakers in Edinburgh and Cardiff is that it is much easier than in Whitehall to bring all the relevant stakeholders round the table, and to grasp the linkages between production, consumption and wellbeing that are at the heart of a rigorous understanding of unsustainable and sustainable forms of development."

I think this is true on a number of levels:

- The dialogue with other nrg4SD members.
- The development of the innovative Wales for Africa programme as a contribution to millennium development goals.
- The commitment to fair trade which led to Wales becoming the first Fair Trade country in the world.

All have helped successive Welsh Governments to develop a greater understanding of sustainable development in the Welsh context. The network discussions were influential in the development of high-level indicators on the economy, social justice, the environment, the ecological footprint and wellbeing – in recognition of the need for metrics against which real performance can be measured - to articulating the values and policy direction needed to underpin those values.

Underneath each of the high level indicators is a set of policy actions to contribute towards 'sustainable resource use', 'sustaining the environment', a 'sustainable economy', a 'sustainable society' and the 'wellbeing of Wales'. Increasingly, it is the latter that is coming to the fore. Wales is already the UK's poorest nation. It has a disproportionate number of people working in the public sector and is therefore at greater risk as public finances dry up.

In 2005, the well regarded and sadly now defunct Sustainable Development Commission worked with governments across the UK to produce *One Future, Different Paths*. This proposed a shared UK understanding of sustainable development. It outlined what we were trying to achieve and the guiding principles we all needed to follow to achieve it. Underpinning principles were:

- **Achieving a Sustainable Economy**
  Building a strong, stable and sustainable economy which provides prosperity and opportunities for all, and in which environmental and social costs fall on those who impose them (Polluter Pays), and efficient resource use is incentivised.

- **Promoting Good Governance**
  Actively promoting effective, participative systems of governance in all levels of society - engaging people's creativity, energy, and diversity.

- **Using Sound Science Responsibly**
  Ensuring policy is developed and implemented on the basis of strong scientific evidence, whilst taking into account scientific uncertainty (through the Precautionary Principle) as well as public attitudes and values.

- **Living Within Environmental Limits**
  Respecting the limits of the planet's environment, resources and biodiversity - to improve our environment and ensure that the natural resources needed for life are unimpaired and remain so for future generations.

- **Ensuring a Strong, Healthy and Just Society**
  Meeting the diverse needs of all people in existing and future communities, promoting personal well being, social cohesion and inclusion, creating equal opportunity for all.

Having expert advice from the Sustainable Development Commission was critical in generating cross party support for this agenda in Wales. With the publication of the Government's current Scheme, *One Wales One Planet* in 2009, a more sustainable Wales was being described as a country which:

- lives within its environmental limits, using only its fair share of the earth's resources so that our ecological footprint is reduced to the global average availability of resources, and we are resilient to the impacts of climate change;

- has healthy, biologically diverse and productive ecosystems that are managed sustainably;

- has a resilient and sustainable economy that is able to develop whilst stabilising, then reducing, its use of natural resources and reducing its contribution to climate change;

- has communities which are safe, sustainable, and attractive places for people to live and work, where people have access to services, and enjoy good health; and

- is a fair, just and bilingual nation, in which citizens of all ages and backgrounds are empowered to determine their own lives, shape their communities and achieve their full potential.

One Wales One Planet was a seminal document. It was the first scheme since the introduction of the duty ten years earlier that articulated a collective commitment from all Ministers to use sustainable development as the central organising principle of government. Previous schemes had had individual actions. This Scheme made an explicit commitment to bring down Wales' ecological footprint to its fair share within the lifetime of a generation. More importantly, as the Welsh Government wrestled with another all party commitment, how to deliver 3 per cent annual greenhouse gas emission reductions, to contribute to UK Climate Change targets by 2050, it found that framing that debate in the context of sustainability created greater political consensus.

To make sustainable development real, it must be outcome focused. To test whether it was delivering different outcomes through the civil service, the Welsh Auditor General decided to investigate whether the concept was adequately embedded in the government's own business practices. There was room for improvement.

Separately, WWF Cymru commissioned a piece of independent research looking at Ministers' policy commitments and whether they were actively delivering on the overarching agenda. Once again there was a mixed picture. However, for the first time, key policy decisions were taken in Wales on waste, on climate change, on retrofitting housing, on planning, on education and on health that were directly linked to sustainable development and were inherently different from decisions being taken elsewhere in the UK.

Three key lessons came out of this experience. First, that the existence of the Duty was supported across all parties and seen as beneficial, as were the regular reporting arrangements which kept the issues in front of members. Secondly, the regional government level which is very close to its population is probably the optimum for delivery of sustainable development. Thirdly, the existing legislation from the Government of Wales Act, although innovative, was inadequate to deliver systemic change. In light of this, in its manifesto for the last election, Welsh Labour outlined its vision for :

"A sustainable Wales to become a 'one planet' nation by putting sustainable development at the heart of government; creating a resilient and sustainable economy that lives within its environmental limits and only using our fair share of the earth's resources to sustain our lifestyles."

That commitment is now being pursued by the present Welsh Government. In June 2011 the First Minister announced that it would, "Legislate to embed sustainable development as the central organising principle in all our actions across government and all public bodies." Crucially, this legislative commitment will be monitored externally by a new independent sustainable development body for Wales following the demise of the UK wide Sustainable Development Commission.

In 2010, in an article *It's Time to get Serious – Why Legislation Is Needed to Make Sustainable Development a Reality in the UK*, Andrea Ross, a co-author in this volume, argued that:

"The UK is now at a stage where specific legislation is required to drive the implementation of sustainable development further forward. Legislation directed at the implementation of sustainable development could potentially address many of the current shortcomings by increasing the priority, support and protection afforded sustainable development across government(s) as a long-term policy objective. Legislation could have a significant symbolic and educational impact in making people understand what is at stake. Moreover, it could crystallise the policy framework already in place and thus, turn what is now, at best, good practice into meaningful legal obligations, supported by monitoring and review mechanisms which impose significant consequences for failure. Finally, legislation could set out how tools such as environmental assessment, procurement practice, research funding and public consultation relate to sustainable development and their role in the overall framework for implementation."

I absolutely agree with this analysis and it is interesting that Andrea's legal journey and my political journey reached a consensus around the same time. The fundamental question for me is how to make sustainable development real in a way that impacts positively on people's lives and leads them to make different and better choices. Clearly an agenda which is ill-defined is not easy for people to rally around. People in Wales generally have a strong social conscience, a strong sense of community and a clear notion of what is fair. All these are pre-requisites for living more sustainably. They are all attributes that would be strengthened under a strong vision for a sustainable Wales, particularly if this was led by government but supported on a cross party basis.

But to be successful we need some fundamental legal changes. Sustainable development will only be made real by defining it in law through which we can establish a process for managing conflicting priorities. This will entail:

- Introducing a legal framework for a sustainable development strategy which requires specified public bodies to refer to it in the context of their sustainable development objectives.

- Auditing its delivery through usual audit mechanisms.

- Establishing the office of a Commissioner for Sustainable Futures as a strong and independent champion of the environment and future generations with significant powers and duties.

A cross party vision was agreed in the National Assembly in 2011:

> "Across society there is recognition of the need to live sustainably and reduce our carbon footprint. People understand how they can contribute to a low carbon, low waste society. These issues are firmly embedded in the curriculum and workplace training. People are taking action to reduce resource use, energy use and waste. They are more strongly focused on environmental, social and economic responsibility, and on local quality of life issues, and there is less emphasis on consumerism. Participation and transparency are key principles of Government at every level, and individuals have become stewards of natural resources."

This is a vision about taking control of our future and our children's future. The question is would you want to live in this future? This is not a question about a physical Wales, much as I could advocate its undoubted charms, including the opening of the Wales coast path in early 2012. This is about a virtual Wales, a country which was at the forefront of the carbon revolution and is now determined to pay its debt by being at the forefront of a new more sustainable world - in recognition of humanity's role as stewards of natural resources.

Mark Twain once said, "If you always do what you've always done, you'll always get what you've always had and that is no longer good enough." I profoundly believe that seeing life though a sustainability lens enables better decision-making and provides the moral compass linking our activities with effects across the world. Wales may be a small country, and it may be the poorest part of the UK, but it has strong community values. It is the first Fair Trade nation in the world. It achieved greater greenhouse gas reductions in 2011 than any other part of the UK. Its recycling performance exceeds any other part of the UK and its new waste legislation is creating green job opportunities. It has had the largest retrofitting housing programme including renewables in disadvantaged areas in the UK. It has continued to focus on fuel poverty when budgets have been removed elsewhere. Its health policy is focused on prevention. Education for Sustainable Development and Global Citizenship is a mandatory element of the Welsh education system at all levels, while its new early years education programme, the Foundation Phase, has sustainability principles throughout. We have to start from where we are and a small, smart, well-connected country with a new devolved governance system may just be the place to test and develop systems, which are fit for the future

I hope that the Wales example will be taken to the Earth Summit and inspire others to embark on the same journey. I have not found another country with this organised commitment to institutionalise sustainability in legislation.

The legislation will take time to make and is anticipated to reach the statute books by 2013. I hope that leading thinkers and practitioners of sustainable change and innovation will share their time, insights, experiences, hopes and fears so that the pathway to country-scale transformation is a shared one. In his masterly essay on *Sustainability in the Age of Austerity*, Tim O'Riordan says:

> "The manner in which sustainability is presented needs to change to fit the national mood of anxiety and frugality over the coming decade. It seems timely to portray a new form of social enterprise economy, where investment in social betterment and individual wellbeing takes on a higher purpose, and the overall value of nature's bounties are included in national accounts. After all, we face a future, not experienced since the end of the last war, when our offspring may be financially worse off than their parents, with fewer jobs of a conventional kind to choose. If this is to be the case, then sustainability needs to embrace the confidence, sense of self worth and capacity to adapt to new forms of employment and living that all people need to experience before they can become true citizens."

This publication and the conference from which it sprang, is part of a two-year process to examine what legislating for sustainable development to be at the heart of government in Wales might look like. It will be different for different people.

Fundamentally, however, it is about securing the best social and economic outcome with the least environmental cost. Our programme brings together policy makers and lawyers to address fundamental issues, and not least how Wales can lead others to a small sustainable world. As Charles Darwin observed, "It is not the strongest of the species that survives, nor the most intelligent, but the one most responsive to change."

Chapter 4
Why legislation is needed
Andrea Ross

The UK and devolved administrations have made considerable efforts over the years to implement sustainable development and this has resulted in some progress.[1] All administrations have regularly produced and reviewed sustainable development strategies and made progress in greening their estates and operations. Indeed, compared with other countries, the UK's progress is enviable.[2] However, these efforts have not been enough to ensure genuine sustainable development[3].

To use one example, while Northern Ireland has yet to produce a set of indicators linked to their sustainable development strategy, Sustainable Development indicators are very well established in rest of the UK. However, analysis reveals that indicator sets are simply not leading to the improvements and progress necessary to move us to a sustainable UK.

Negative trends year after year in the indicators sets is not influencing government behaviour. For example the 2011 booklet *Sustainable Development Indicators for Wales* reports that 50 per cent of the indicators still show either little or no change or a clear deterioration since the relevant base year (2002-03 or 2003-04), and for another 7 per cent there remain insufficient data. Wales has been producing indicator sets for over a decade, yet still shows no progress for more than half of its indicators, including key environmental indicators:

• Short-term changes in bird populations
• Ecological impacts of pollution from nitrates and acidity
• The waste arising by sector
• The chemical quality of rivers
• Greenhouse gas emissions
• Priority habitat status
• Household waste
• The number of people walking or cycling and using public transport.[4]

Wales' situation is mirrored across the UK and the EU. The European Commission's 2009 review notes that, despite considerable efforts to include action for sustainable development in major EU policy areas, unsustainable trends persist.[5] There is no sense of urgency about the challenges facing the world. Minute improvements are celebrated, not getting worse is considered progress and even bad news is not enough to compel action. This is indicative of the low priority afforded sustainable development, the sustainable development strategies and the indicators within the administrations.

Research shows that the UK strategies all lack influence and their use in practice is sporadic at best. There are problems with the interpretation of the term 'sustainable development', with the process of developing and reviewing the impact of sustainable development strategies, and also with how such strategies are used in decision making more generally[6].

Inconsistent interpretations of the term 'sustainable development' in the UK include:

- The use of sustainable development in a standard list of cross-cutting themes such as equality, social justice and bilingualism. This confusion is exacerbated by doubts whether sustainable development should be given 'primacy' over other issues.

- Tokenistic use of sustainable development with no meaningful explanation of what this entails.

- Confusing terminology related to environmental sustainability, longevity and robustness.

- A limited number of defined action/processes and responsibilities related to sustainable development and a lack of urgency in the message about the need for change.

The UK Coalition Government's use of the term is particularly muddled. It regularly uses the terms 'sustainable' and 'sustainable development' inconsistently and, arguably, inappropriately. For example, the 2011 Budget stated that the Government would introduce into the land use planning system "a powerful new presumption in favour of sustainable development, so that the default is 'yes'."[7]

Unfortunately much of this inconsistency is an inherent and accepted part of a balancing process used in the weak but favoured 'three pronged' approach to sustainable development. This is where economic, environmental and social factors are balanced against one another and little priority is given to long-term concerns or to the Earth's limits or carrying capacity.

The acceptability and usefulness of any strategy is dependent on its legitimacy. While the content is important, the procedures used for its development, use and review are equally important. Thus, a strategy whose development process makes sense to the public and stakeholders will be widely accepted as legitimate.

However, in practice the development and deployment of sustainable development strategies have been ad hoc and inconsistent. There have been some impressive processes. For example, the former Sustainable Development Commission in Scotland provided thorough annual reviews of Scotland's progress towards the targets, indicators and objectives set out in its strategy. However, these were dropped when the Scottish Government joined the UK government in ceasing to fund the Sustainable Development Commission without any obvious replacement.

There are two other key procedural factors missing from most of the processes used by the UK administrations for developing their strategies which affect the acceptance, accountability and legitimacy of the strategy.[8] To be effective, responsibility for producing and reviewing the sustainable development strategy should be placed at the highest level of government and not in the hands of a less influential 'department of the environment'. This makes the leader responsible and accountable for the success or failure of the strategy across government and in turn, keeps the leader interested and informed. At present, in the UK, only Northern Ireland places responsibility for its sustainable development strategy with the Office of the First Minister and Deputy First Minister.

Sustainable development also needs a legislative underpinning to increase its status, legitimacy and relevance. At present in the UK, such statutory backing only exists in Wales. Arguably it is this legislative commitment that has enabled Wales to become the most committed to sustainable development. That said, even in Wales, the process set out in the Government of Wales Act 2006 is too vague with, for example, no details provided about who to consult or how to consult.

Across the UK, decisions continue to be made with little regard to the principles in the relevant sustainable development strategy. As Blair and Evans put it:

> "For sustainability to be mainstreamed, the frameworks of corporate management, the processes and specific tools (targets and indicators), audit, review and inspection procedures all need to be appropriately aligned and geared to a common sustainability set of criteria".[9]

Currently this is not the case. There are numerous examples of innovation in relation to promoting leadership, stakeholder involvement, and policy integration. They include:

- Training for sustainable development.
- High level committees, for example in Cabinet or among senior officials.
- Action plans.
- Efforts in sustainable procurement.
- Institutional developments such as the creation of the Department of Energy and Climate Change.
- Legal duties such as those imposed in the various planning Acts.
- Reporting and review processes such as those provided by the annual progress reports on the sustainable development indicators.
- The Sustainable Development Commission.
- The Environmental Audit Committee of the House of Commons.[10]

However, these sustainable development tools are inconsistently used. For instance, indicators are often of little policy relevance, as they are not explicitly linked to clear objectives in the national strategy. Budget decisions, such as those capping environmental taxes, continue to be made for short-term electoral gains. Sadly, there are also examples of useful sustainable development mechanisms falling into disuse or being discontinued.

Some of these losses are significant and several are retrograde steps. Examples include the failure of the Scottish Government to consult widely on its *Economic Strategy*, the loss of both the Scottish and UK cabinet committees on sustainable development and the decision to cease the funding of the Sustainable Development Commission.

Thus, the UK's failure to deliver sustainable development can largely be attributed to three key factors. First, while much of the regulatory architecture is in place for moving towards a sustainable UK, this architecture lacks a clear and consistent interpretation of sustainable development and fails to prioritise the Earth's limits. Second, sustainable development itself, the sustainable development strategies and other mechanisms lack legitimacy, influence and status in decision making. Finally, good practice and institutional innovations are not suitably supported and leaders are too easily swayed by misguided short-termism.

Research into sustainable development broadly agrees that three significant changes are required for effective implementation.[11] First, there should be a cultural acceptance and understanding that prioritises operating within the Earth's limits and thinking about the long-term effects of policies and decisions. The success of this first change depends on the second significant change, which is the full integration of environmental protection concerns, and more broadly, sustainable development, into all forms of policy and decision making. Both changes need to be supported by a third change, effective leadership for sustainable development.

All of these changes need to be supported by a strong institutional and legislative framework and in many ways this is where the UK's architecture for sustainable development is currently lacking. Change is possible and what follows is an admittedly legal perspective on how to address each of the three interrelated changes needed to actually start delivering sustainable development.

Improving the understanding of sustainable development

The current inconsistent interpretation of sustainable development can be traced to the balancing process inherent in weak sustainability. Sustainable development is popular with policy makers and has proved its resilience as a policy objective in the UK. However, the favoured three-pronged approach to delivering all aspects of sustainable development at the same time provides little guidance on how to make hard choices and what needs to be prioritised to ensure we can meet the needs of the future. Weak sustainability does not address the ecological, economic, and social realities facing the UK and the world. It does not acknowledge the scale of the challenges, the urgency needed to tackle them and the level of co-ordination required.[12]

Sustainable development needs to be redefined in a meaningful way, with clear limits and priorities that focus on ecological sustainability and wellbeing instead of economic growth. Moreover, there is also a case for raising the legal status of ecological sustainability to a fundamental legal principle that is protected by society and the legal system in a similar way to 'justice' [13]. In turn, there is a case for raising the status of sustainable development to become the central organising principle of government.

Ideally, a new UK-wide framework is needed, that sets out a co-ordinated and agreed vision of sustainable development among the four UK administrations, and that includes clear priorities that are easily understood. Modern strategies such as the *Earth Charter* and *One Wales, One Planet* show that there is a growing shift in favour of more ecologically based interpretations of sustainable development. The individual administrations would then need to expand on this framework to produce more detailed strategies for their own jurisdictions and competences. Ideally, the production of these new strategies would be the responsibility of Ministers at the highest level, in order to ensure that the process and results retain political significance and are widely accepted and promoted across government.

As a consequence of this approach, specific mechanisms are necessary to establish the carrying capacity of the Earth's ecosystems. Such mechanisms include stabilisation wedges, environmental assessment and ecological footprints. These need to be continuously developed, refined and improved, especially in relation to knowledge management. These mechanisms must remain firmly focused on ecological limits and be kept separate from broader sustainable development tools such as the strategies themselves, sustainability appraisals and the wider impact assessment and sustainable development duties. It is essential that these latter mechanisms also address social and economic concerns.

Once limits are understood - that is, in terms of the carrying capacity of one or more of the Earth's ecosystems - it is then the role of sustainable development to promote and encourage social and economic development within these limits. With ecological sustainability at its core, sustainable development has the capacity to set meaningful objectives, duties and policy rules. It can also provide boundaries for decision-making. These roles are already present in recent UK and devolved legislation, which impose duties on public bodies to "contribute to the achievement of sustainable development".

Increasing the status of sustainable development through legislation

The next question is how to ensure more consistency in the application of sustainable development in wider decision-making. Even if a new vision based on ecological sustainability is widely accepted, and accompanied by a clear message and explicit links in a strategy, discrepancies are still likely to emerge within an administration regarding delivery and compliance with procedures. There will always be pressure from those pushing short-term agendas.

Varying levels of priority for the sustainable development objectives have a knock-on effect on mechanisms such as sustainable development action plans, indicators, public service agreement targets and various appraisal tools. Indeed, while there is plenty of evidence of holistic thinking and good practice across the UK, there has not been the necessary groundswell of public and institutional support needed to apply sustainable development consistently and make it the cultural norm both inside and outside government.

Success also depends on leadership and a long-term view which addresses both consumption and supply. The current policy approach supported by only minimal legislation has not proved capable of resisting electoral short-termism. Nor has it supported and promoted real leaders in sustainable development. The more we erode the Earth's carrying capacity, the more the ability of leaders to provide answers to economic and social crises diminishes.

Sustainable development has proved itself to be valuable policy tool and worthy of legislative backing in the UK. Legislation could compel compliance and adherence to best practice. It could also promote consistency in the interpretation of sustainable development and use of the Sustainable Development Scheme or Strategy. It could also create a meaningful framework for decision-making, while ensuring that this framework is iterative and flexible.

A UK-wide statute on sustainable development that binds both central and devolved administrations alike is unfeasible following devolution. However, it would not be out of step with modern UK legal culture for the UK, Scotland, Wales and Northern Ireland legislatures to enact their own legislation on sustainable development.

A key issue for legislators to decide is which legislative model for sustainable development is appropriate for their jurisdiction. In the context of the UK and the devolved administrations, three possible models exist that reflect different levels of political commitment. The first focuses on creating binding legal procedures considered vital to implement sustainable development fully, such as the production of a strategy, wide consultation, and reports on progress.

However, procedures alone will not necessarily deliver a cultural change within governments. The second model enhances the status of the sustainable development strategy by introducing a substantive duty across government to ensure that all its activities are consistent with the objectives and principles set out in the sustainable development strategy. This approach gives the strategy legal status, provides a clear point of reference for those bodies with obligations relating to sustainable development and, generally, improves the understanding of the term. It also ensures more consistency in its use and application.

Yet, this approach does not explicitly set out the role of sustainable development in the workings of government. This omission misses out on important symbolic benefits and fails to address directly any inconsistencies in the interpretation and application of sustainable development.
If the real cultural change described earlier is actually going to happen, then governments need to legislate to make sustainable development the central

organising principle of governance. This third model requires two additional legislative provisions. First, there must be a clear declaration of purpose by government about the role of sustainable development in all its activities. The statement in *One Wales, One Planet* works well as a declaration of purpose:

> "Sustainable development (the process that leads to Wales becoming a sustainable nation) will be the central organising principle of Government, and we will encourage and enable others to embrace sustainable development as their central organising principle".[14]

Secondly, the legislation must impose meaningful substantive duties on all government bodies. These duties should do more than simply require them to 'have regard to' or 'take account of' sustainable development. Sustainable development needs to be more than a material consideration, or one objective to be balanced against others. Helpfully, there is precedent in previous statutes of a better approach. For example, the Planning and Compulsory Purchase Act 2004 in relation to development planning provides in s. 39(2) that:

> "The person or body must exercise [their functions] with the objective of contributing to the achievement of sustainable development".

Another useful form of words is in the Local Government in Scotland Act 2003 s. 1(5) which provides that

> "The local authority shall discharge its duties under this section in a way which contributes to the achievement of sustainable development".

Both phrasings are strong enough to potentially give the provisions the status of legal rule and hence, truly provide a framework for all decision-making across government.

In the past, this author has been unconvinced of the value of legislating to define sustainable development or of referring to certain underlying principles such as good governance or sound science[15]. More recently however, some more specific definitions/interpretations have been set out which, while still retaining some flexibility, provide more detailed limits than the oft quoted Brundtland definition -"development that meets the needs of the present while not compromising the ability of future generations to meet their own needs." [16]

Moreover, certain clear priorities set out in the legislation would be very helpful for promoting a consistent approach. A useful sample definition was provided in Regulation (EC) No 2493/2000 of the European Parliament and of the Council of 7 November 2000 on measures to promote the full integration of the environmental dimension in the development process of developing countries. This provides that:

> "For the purposes of this Regulation 'sustainable development' means the improvement of the standard of living and welfare of the relevant populations within the limits of the capacity of the ecosystems by maintaining natural assets and their biological diversity for the benefit of present and future generations."[17]

This definition makes no mention of economic growth and would be useful in adding clarity and priorities to the interpretation of sustainable development. More research is needed on how best to deliver these more substantive goals while still retaining the flexibility needed to allow sustainable development to evolve over time.

Finally, implementation of sustainable development thus far has been a staged process in the UK and elsewhere. There is no reason to believe it will not continue to be so. While legislation which adopts the Sustainable Development Commission's vision of sustainable development as the central organising principle of governance in the UK is desperately needed and, arguably, is the best way forward, it may take the UK administrations a while to be willing to give this legislative backing. It will likely take the UK courts longer still to recognise such a change in priorities.

Legal formalisation would raise the status of the sustainable development strategy and of sustainable development itself. It would also upgrade the framework approach from a nice idea to a legal obligation. Failure to produce a strategy or to observe the legislated procedural requirements would not only be subject to judicial review, but would also attract considerable public attention and thus, significantly improve scrutiny and accounting on sustainable development. This would also provide vital support to sustainable leadership, promote education for sustainable development, and raise the status of both the strategy and sustainable development more generally in the public eye.

Overcoming poor leadership

Poor leadership is the third crucial failing influencing the UK's lack of success in implementing sustainable development[18]. However, our leaders also need legal and institutional support. In 2011, the UK Coalition government discontinued the requirement for all government departments to produce sustainable development action plans with no obvious replacement. Together with its decision to cease funding the Sustainable Development Commission, this demonstrated how even the most effective mechanisms need protection from political short-termism. Our leaders need support to avoid opting for easy short term solutions and to consider long-term challenges.

The solutions for addressing the previous two failings may also improve leadership in sustainable development. A clear definition will increase understanding of sustainable development among the wider community and, as such, increase the number of sustainably literate leaders available. Moreover, while a lack of sustainable development leadership is often the underlying cause of inconsistency and regressive decision-making, the converse is also true. Legislation could be used to compel leaders to produce strategies, use certain means of stakeholder involvement, and explicitly consider environmental limits and inequities. It could also be used to support sustainable development leadership by compelling regular cross-administration working and even go so far as to impose a duty on all government public bodies to make sustainable development the organising principle of government.

An abundance of good and evolving practice exists. Unfortunately, good practice is being ignored, abandoned or revoked often for short-term objectives. This could be made more difficult. The law offers several different means for supporting good practice aimed at the long-term sustainable development of the UK, and its component nations.

Notes

1   More detail on many of the ideas in this paper can be found in Ross, A *Sustainable Development Law in the UK: From Rhetoric to Reality*, Earthscan/Routledge, and, in particular, chapters 11 and 14, 2012; and in Ross, A. 'It's time to get serious – why legislation is needed to make sustainable development a reality in the UK', *Sustainability*, Vol. 2, no 4, pp1101-1127, 2010.

2   Swanson, D. and Pinter, L., (2007) 'Governance strategies for National Sustainable Development strategies, chapter 4, in OECD *Institutionalizing Sustainable Development*, OECD, 2007; Ross, A (2012) *Sustainable Development Law in the UK: From Rhetoric to Reality*, Earthscan/Routledge, p262.

3   Porritt, J. 'The standing of sustainable development in government', http://www.jonathonporritt.com/pages/2009/11/the_standing_of_sustainable_de.html. 2009.

4   Statistics for Wales, 2011.

5   European Commission, p.15, 2009; Eurostat, pp.9-10, 2009.

6   Ross, A., 'It's time to get serious – why legislation is needed to make sustainable development a reality in the UK', *Sustainability*, vol 2, no 4, pp1101-1127, 2010; Flynn, A., Marsden, T., Netherwood, A. and Pitts, R., *Final Report, The Sustainable Development Effectiveness Report for the Welsh Assembly*, Welsh Government, 2008.

7   HM Treasury, *Budget 2011*, HC 836, Stationary Office, p. 3., 2011.

8   Swanson, D., Pinter, L., Bregha, F., Volkery, A. and Jacob, K., *National Strategies for Sustainable Development: Challenges, Approaches and Innovations in Strategic and Co-ordinated Action*, IISD, Stratos Inc, Environmental Policy Research Centre, 2004.

9   Blair, F. and Evans, B. (2004) *Seeing the Bigger Picture*, Sustainable Development Commission, Newcastle, p. 41, 2004.

10   Ross, *A Sustainable Development Law in the UK: From Rhetoric to Reality*, Earthscan/Routledge, 2012.

11   *Ibid.*, chapter 3.

12   *Sustainable Development: Third Annual Assessment of Progress by the Scottish Government*, p.41, 2009.

13   Bosselmann, K., *The Principle of Sustainability – Transforming Law and Governance*, Ashgate, 2008.

14   Welsh Government, *One Wales: One Planet, a New Sustainable Development Scheme for Wales*, p. 13, 2009.

15   Ross, A., 'Why legislate for sustainable development? An examination of sustainable development provisions in UK and Scottish statutes', *Journal of Environmental Law*, vol 20, no 1, pp35-68, 2008.

16   World Commission on Environment and Development, *Our Common Future* (The Brundtland Report), 1987.

17   Regulation (EC) No 2493/2000 of the European Parliament and of the Council of 7 November 2000 on measures to promote the full integration of the environmental dimension in the development process of developing countries [2000] OJ L288, Article 2. Note that this regulation was repealed by Regulation (EC) No 1905/2006 of the European Parliament and of the Council of 18 December 2006 establishing a financing instrument for development co-operation [2006] OJ L348, which contains no such definition of sustainable development.

18   MacNeill, J., 'Leadership for sustainable development', in *Institutionalising Sustainable Development*, OECD Sustainable Development Studies, OECD Publishing, 2007; Parkin, S., *The Positive Deviant – Sustainability Leadership in a Perverse World*, Earthscan Publications, 2010; and Rayment, J.J. and Smith, J.A., *Misleadership: Prevalence, Causes and Consequences*, Gower Publishing, 2010.

Chapter 5
A crucial step in Wales' devolution journey
Peter Davies

The Welsh Government's duty to promote sustainable development has been a distinctive dimension of the devolution journey. It is supported across the political spectrum and is a source of pride in the National Assembly. It is also recognised internationally as being a leading example in the integration of sustainable development within governance structures. The current duty is set out in the Government of Wales Act 2006, and covers three main elements:

1. To make a scheme setting out how Welsh Ministers propose to promote sustainable development in the exercise of their functions – currently *One Wales One Planet*.

2. To publish an annual report setting out how the proposals in the scheme have been implemented – the latest published last October with an independent commentary.[1]

3. Following an election to the National Assembly, to publish a report containing an assessment of how effective the scheme has been in promoting sustainable development. The latest report was completed by PriceWaterhouseCoopers and debated in plenary session at the end of January 2012.[2]

These elements have provided an important strategic framework. However, they fall short of a duty on the Welsh Government to actually promote sustainable development. Meanwhile the duty falls only on the Welsh Government and does not include the devolved public sector in Wales within its scope.

Indeed, the various independent reviews have consistently highlighted the weaknesses in the model which requires the production of a 'scheme' to promote sustainable development. The scheme document and annual reports have been seen to operate in a parallel universe to the programme of government. Departments have been able merely to 'cherry pick' and 'cut and paste' more sustainable elements of their programmes to be included in the scheme and associated reports.

Having said that, there is no doubt that the current Sustainable Development Scheme *One Wales: One Planet*, published in May 2009, represented a significant step forward, with the government voluntarily making the decision to adopt sustainable development as its central organising principle. The concept of a central organising principle is becoming well established across government. Nonetheless, and understandably, there remains a significant gap between the adoption of the principle and its implementation as a way of decision making across government.

The introduction of a Sustainable Development Bill as part of the present Welsh Government's legislative programme stresses that sustainability lies at the heart of its policy-making. The Bill will aim to promote economic, social and environmental well being and to enhance people's quality of life in Wales. Critically, it will refer to sustainability not so much as a green idea but more about defining the long-term development path for our nation.

The Bill will also establish an independent sustainable development body, to provide advice and guidance on sustainable development in a way that best reflects Welsh interests and needs. This will confirm in legislation the decision of the previous administration to maintain an independent Commissioner function following the UK Government's decision to end the UK Sustainable Development Commission.

The organisations covered by the Bill will include Local Authorities and National Park Authorities, the NHS and Local Health Boards, fire and rescue authorities, colleges, universities, National Museums and Libraries, along with a number of bodies that the Welsh Government funds.

The first public discussion document setting out the Government's initial thinking for the new Bill was launched by the Minister in November 2011[3]. This paper will be revised to form the basis of a more formal consultation leading to a White Paper in autumn 2012. In turn, this will set out the proposed purpose and intent of the Sustainable Development Bill, the case for change, the preferred option and the evidence base underpinning it. A Bill will then be introduced into the Assembly in Autumn 2013. The process will have to address a number of key questions:

• How should legislation bring about a step change in sustainable development?
• What does the public sector, with sustainable development as its central organising principle, look like and how does it operate?
• What new duties or powers might bring that about?
• What should be included in the body of the Bill and what might be included in any statutory or non-statutory guidance that might accompany the Bill, once passed?
• How best can we ensure compliance with the Bill?

- What should be the role of the independent sustainable development body?

However, the biggest challenge is the practical definition and application of the slippery concept of sustainable development. How can this be achieved in a way that focuses effort on making a difference on the ground rather than tick box exercises and added bureaucracy?

The current discussion document focuses on governance for sustainable development. It sets out an approach to decision-making that takes account of the long-term, demands integration, reduces complexity, encourages joined-up thinking and active participation. It proposes that such an approach would focus on the hard decisions about:

- How to make best use of resources to maximise people's wellbeing over the long term, prioritising prevention rather than tackling symptoms.
- Focusing on the early identification of the causes of problems and tackling these rather than tackling the symptoms at a later date.
- Ensuring that decisions do not impose unintended costs elsewhere, through integrating required economic, social and environmental outcomes into all decisions.
- Thinking long-term so that decisions today do not leave future generations picking up the cost.

All of these are obviously desirable and important principles if we are to ensure that the public sector becomes more effective in governing for long-term well being. However, a real challenge is how to make this happen in a way that passes the 'pub test' in focusing on outcomes.

One key point in Wales' favour is that despite our leadership rhetoric on sustainable development, we are far from alone in trying to address the issue of governance for the long term. The United Nations Earth Summit Rio+20 being held in June 2012 has governance for sustainable development as a key theme. Organisations such as the World Futures Council and the Foundation for Democracy and Sustainable Development are working with countries and states on models of governance for the future and calling for the establishment of a UN Commissioner for Future Generations.[4] There are real opportunities for Wales in being part of this global development, not least in setting out our stall to the increasing number of global companies which have similar commitments.

The concept of an independent Commissioner is central to proposals in the Welsh Bill.

The Welsh Government will legislate to set up an independent body on sustainable development to meet Welsh needs. The role of an independent Commissioner is well established in the devolved governance model, with our Commissioners for children, older people and most recently the Welsh language. It will be important to draw from these models and also consider the opportunities of shared approaches to fulfilling the respective duties. The Sustainable Development Bill discussion paper sets out a number of possible options for the new body, for example:

- An Ombudsman serving citizens, enforcing rights and dealing with specific case work following the model of the Hungarian Commissioner for Future Generations.

- A Welsh Government funded body, with a Commissioner appointed by and reporting to, but independent from, Welsh Ministers, set up to advise, guide and challenge the Welsh Government and the devolved public sector on sustainable development.

- A Commission appointed by the National Assembly, independent from Welsh Government, focusing on scrutiny and holding the Welsh Government and the devolved public sector to account on sustainable development.

In looking at models in other countries, it is interesting to consider the recommendations from a 2007 Parliamentary Inquiry in Australia. Although never enacted, it was well researched and continues to be referenced as an important document. The clearly set out the role of an independent Commission as envisaged under the Sustainable Development Bill, including:

- Defining the sustainability goals for Australia.
- Creating an aspirational Charter, supported by an implementation plan containing targets.
- Evaluating progress towards meeting national sustainability goals, objectives and targets and reporting on this to both Houses of the Federal Parliament.
- Conducting inquiries into sustainability matters, recommending remedial measures for unsustainable practices and gaps in policies acknowledging those that are sustainable.
- Reviewing (when necessary) national sustainability goals, objectives and targets, building and strengthening partnerships with government, industry and the community (nationally and internationally).
- Influencing and guiding government, industry and the wider community.
- Advancing sustainability outcomes by collecting, maintaining and disseminating information on sustainability, including national performance statistics.

This model provides a basis for considering how a similar body in Wales could fulfil these functions. It could help bring a focus on outcomes to what can be a very technocratic approach to influencing decision-making in the public sector.

A new cross sector Commission body could have responsibility for consulting to establish the key goals and sustainable development indicators for Wales, making recommendations to Government and monitoring progress across the public sector. It could also have a duty to demonstrate their contribution to achieving the goals and improving performance against the key indicators.

Such an approach would put sustainable development indicators centre stage rather than being peripheral to government programmes. It would also underpin and strengthen the concept of the Sustainable Development Charter which was introduced by Welsh Government in 2011. Each signatory organisation would have to demonstrate their contribution to the achievement of the goals and measures.

As we shape the proposals for the White Paper it is important we focus on the outcomes we want to achieve rather than process. Whatever the detail of the model that emerges, it is essential the Sustainable Development Bill establishes the means to achieve a better sense of our long-term path as a nation. We need a wider set of goals to measures policy performance that just growth in GDP. The White Paper should also provide a compelling vision that can mobilise people into a shared responsibility for action.

Notes

1   The Annual Report is available at:
    http://wales.gov.uk/topics/sustainabledevelopment/publications/annualreport1011/?lang=en

2   Effectiveness Review of the Sustainable Development Scheme Final Report is available at:
    http://wales.gov.uk/topics/sustainabledevelopment/publications/effectivenessreview2012/?lang=en

3   Available at: http://wales.gov.uk/topics/sustainabledevelopment/sdbill/?lang=en

4   See http://www.worldfuturecouncil.org/ and http://www.fdsd.org/

Chapter 6
Main event or bureaucratic sideshow?
Tim Peppin

Will the Welsh Government's commitment to make sustainable development the 'central organising principle' for all public bodies lead to significant change in the way local authorities operate? Or will it generate an additional layer of bureaucratic form filling and auditing?

Amongst other things the Sustainability Bill will introduce the 'central organising principle' requirement. Local authorities are already subject to a wide range of legislation that should force them to consider sustainable development issues in their activities. A report produced for Welsh Local Government Association by PricewaterhouseCoopers has set out these existing legal duties.[1] So will the Bill really make any substantial difference? There are at least five considerations:

1. On a general level, making anything a legal requirement helps to raise its profile. It gives a clear signal that a subject is seen as significant.

2. As a result of the work that has to go into Bill preparation a level of rigour is required, setting out exactly what is required.

3. By embracing sustainability 'in the round' there is the potential to give greater coherence to the existing legal requirements, and perhaps to remove some existing duties.

4. As a legal requirement, the issue holds greater sway in discussions about the allocation and prioritisation of resources. It also offers some protection, and hopefully stimulates innovative thinking, at a time of financial cutbacks.

5. Finally, there are well understood mechanisms to deal with failure/breaches.

The fact that the Sustainability Bill will apply to *all* public bodies also makes a difference. The very nature of sustainable development means that actions are required across a range of organisations and legislation focused solely on local authorities is unlikely to be sufficient. Indeed, if the Bill is to be effective it must challenge some current institutional arrangements that act as blocks on organisations adopting more sustainable approaches. Some areas are already experimenting with a 'total place' approach where all the public funds being spent in an area are pooled. Public and other organisations work together to eliminate wasteful duplication and ensure more efficient and effective use of the resources.

Other 'institutional' barriers include annual financial accounting practices which tend to discourage consideration of lifetime costs. They also make it hard to introduce invest to save and preventative initiatives due to the upfront spend required. Worse still, they can encourage wasteful use of resources at the end of the financial year. Organisations often take short-term measures to ensure their budget is fully spent, to 'protect' it for the next year.

The political term of office can also act as a substantial constraint on the pursuit of goals that by their very nature have a payback only over the long term. However, joint work between local authorities and the Welsh Government on long term investments in waste facilities and on a borrowing initiative to improve the highway network show that commitments over a 20-25 year timescale are possible.

If sustainable development is really to become the central organising principle for public bodies, almost by definition the Bill must call for an approach that is *community-centred* and involves residents. The essence of the Bill must be capable of being easily understood by the public and accountabilities for compliance must be clear.

The Bill needs to call for evidence that underpins important decisions by public bodies to be open and transparent. It should be necessary to show that social, economic and environmental implications have been fully thought through and that views of stakeholder and other interested parties have been given due consideration in coming to a decision. The proposal for a new sustainable development body as part of the Bill could be significant for some of the higher profile issues, given the scope for disagreement on what is the most sustainable long-term path.

Towards a sustainable public service

So what might we expect to see in the public sector in the wake of new legislation on sustainability? Public bodies will need to ensure that all staff have a basic understanding of sustainable development.[2] Some key staff in all service areas will need to be trained to a higher level. There is huge scope for collective training sessions for public sector bodies, working with the further and higher education sectors and other training providers to meet these needs.

Such joint training will facilitate a more integrated approach to the analysis of problems and encourage jointly managed consultation exercises. In turn, this should result in jointly developed 'business' cases identifying radical new ways of tackling issues, with the active involvement of local residents. They should be based on enhanced cost benefit analyses, undertaken *across* organisations and taking account of issues such as the social return on investments. In framing responses, pooled budgets and joint procurement should become automatic, drawing in knowledge, resources and expertise from social enterprises in the third sector, and from the private sector as appropriate.

Over time, 'system savings' from more effective use of resources and successful preventative action can be directed to greatest needs, with appropriate democratic oversight. Finally, reporting of these activities and progress will need to reflect - and publicise - this approach. Expansion from 'simple' annual financial accounts to public sector 'triple bottom line' analysis will make reports more interesting to the wider public, creating its own pressures and momentum. Indeed, some argue that more important than triple bottom line reporting is 'triple top line' planning where the social, economic and environmental considerations are considered and consulted upon upstream, not simply reviewed after the event.

Support for local authorities

Since 2007, with financial support from the Welsh Government, the Welsh Local Government Association has been supporting local authorities to take more sustainable approaches to their services. A range of material produced as part of this project is freely available on the WLGA website.[3] It includes 'Futures' modules developed by Netherwood Sustainable Futures, helping authorities to build longer term considerations into today's planning. To date over 800 local authority officers and members have been engaged in events and activities. However, to put this in perspective, this represents around half of one per cent of the local government workforce in Wales.

In 2011-12 a more focused approach was adopted. Instead of attempting to spread sustainable development resources thinly across all authorities, a concentrated effort was made in a more limited number of authorities. Following a competitive bidding exercise, Swansea was selected to receive intensive support across a range of its activities. The intention is to build a critical mass of sustainable development based activity which will inform thinking on what it means in practice to make it 'the central organising principle'.

With the support of Swansea's Leader, Chief Executive and Management Team, consultants engaged under the project are working with the authority on a range of different fronts. These include looking at reporting arrangements, 'translating' Futures work to a local level to identify spatial implications, working with adult social services and also setting up round table sessions with a range of external experts to have a fresh look at the 'wicked issues' that are currently creating serious budget pressures. Efficiency measures are being looked at in terms of how they relate to climate change and can contribute to mitigation and adaptation. In addition, key processes that are at the heart of the operation any local authority - including business planning and asset management - are being reviewed to ensure that sustainable development considerations feature explicitly.

An 'open book' approach is being taken so that local authorities and other public bodies with an interest can benefit from the learning and, where appropriate sit in on sessions – not only to learn but also to offer additional insight and experience.

None of this is easy. If it was many of these measures would already be commonplace. However, the weight of existing systems can be crushing and good practice in sustainable development is often the exception rather than the norm.

Incremental improvement is not an option given the seriousness and proximity of some of the 'futures' issues we really should be addressing today. If the situation is to change we need to be prepared to be bold and take some risks with the Bill. With such an all-encompassing issue as sustainable development it would be easy to produce a Bill that is either so high level that is has little practical impact, or one that attempts to pin so many issues down that it ends up generating an industry of report writing and form filling, with all the associated audit and inspection.

The prize will be to create a piece of legislation where the duty on public bodies is easy to understand and encourages more 'joined-up' approaches across the public sector. It must enable open and transparent assessment of how well a body (or bodies collectively) has taken all necessary factors into consideration before taking decisions. And crucially, it must result in practice that steers our economy and society into activities that are resource efficient and within environmental limits, whilst also delivering what local residents regard as improvements in their quality of life.

That is a tall order. But the preparatory work by the Welsh Government is being undertaken in a thorough, enthusiastic and committed way. The stakes are high but there is real potential to elevate sustainable development to its rightful position and to make a genuine difference.

Achieving this will require that sustainable development considerations are at the forefront in all strategic discussions. One example is the identification of collaborative opportunities in light of the Simpson report. This called for a review of what local government functions are best carried out at which level – whether 'national, local or regional'. These discussions need to be held between organisations, and not purely across local government, to ensure all options are considered. Likewise, local government needs to be involved in planning for the new Single Body that will bring together the Environment Agency, the Countryside Council for Wales and the Forestry Commission. Sustainable development will also be required by the European Commission to be at the heart of the post 2013 European programmes. It will need to be done in a meaningful way and not seen as 'another box to be completed'.

In the words of Machiavelli, "never great was anything achieved without danger". There are many risks and potential pitfalls in this current endeavour. However, now is a time for boldness, and a willingness to challenge the way we do things. 'Business as usual' is not an option. There is a real opportunity to make sustainable development the 'main event'.

Notes

1   See http://www.wlga.gov.uk/english/archive-of-reports9/wlga-pwc-report-sustainable-development-local-authority-duties-and-responsibilities/

2   This should be no different in principle to health and safety, equalities, codes of conduct and other areas where employers have legal obligations to ensure their staff know what is required of them. Indeed, sustainable development should embrace and give structure to all such responsibilities.

3   See: http://www.wlga.gov.uk/english/sustainable-development-framework/.

Chapter 7
Public health and sustainable development
Stephen Palmer

Sustainable development provides a brilliant paradigm for thinking about the health of the public. For understandable political reasons, Government tends to see public health as the sum total of unhealthy individual behaviours. It follows that the route to change is through public health practitioners and the NHS getting the message out to people better.

However, despite enormous publicity and much exhortation by GPs and hospital doctors Wales is doing badly in terms of health indicators. Over half the population is obese or significantly overweight. A quarter smoke, and only a third eat enough fruit and vegetables and take enough exercise. Nearly half drink above the daily alcohol guidelines and over a quarter binge drink. A third of Welsh women are smokers when they become pregnant.[1]

The ecological health map shown on the following page demonstrates that focussing on the individual alone is unlikely to be effective.[2] This is because health drivers do not operate just at the level of the individual. Crucially, they include wider societal and environmental influences as well.

Recent history has shown that Government can act effectively to address some of these contextual factors and change the pressures on individuals to behave unhealthily. Examples range from legislation on seat belts to smoking in public places. Other potential areas for intervention are currently too hot to handle. They include regulating the fat and sugar content of foods, alcohol pricing and transport policies.

The sustainable development paradigm offers a way of integrating understanding through the levels and across the economic, social and environmental domains. It addresses the challenge of creating healthy places, where health is not the ultimate goal though a necessary means to attaining flourishing communities. Tony Blair reflected this vision in his introduction to the UK Government's sustainable development strategy *Securing the Future* in 2005:

> "No community, here or overseas, wants to be faced with problems which lead to them becoming caught in a cycle of degradation and poverty, with a consequent lack of community pride in their area, poor environmental

quality and health, high crime and unemployment levels, and multiple inequalities... Our aim is to create sustainable communities — places where people want to live and work, now and in the future... we aim to improve the lives of people in deprived communities and socially excluded groups who experience poor quality of life, including poor local environmental quality and poor access to services."[3]

Health map for the local human habitat

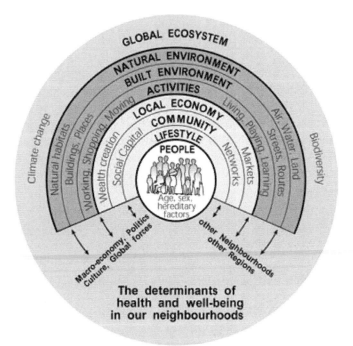

The determinants of health and well-being in our neighbourhoods

Within this paradigm, the public health policy should use all the influences that impact on health, from the individual through to the family, neighbourhood, regional, national, and global.

Threats to sustainability

There is a broad international consensus on the main threats to sustainable development. These combine economic and social trends with environmental threats:

- Demographic, economic and social trends - an ageing population, worklessness, regional imbalances, as well as poverty and social exclusion, health inequalities and 'egoistic individualism'.

- Environmental threats - climate change and global warming, extreme weather events, natural disasters, potential threats from persistent toxic chemicals, resistance to antibiotics, food safety and security, loss of biodiversity and emergence of zoonotic diseases.

Individually, each of these threats can be reasonably well understood. However, the real challenge is to understand and predict the effects of the complex interplay of the economic, social and environmental factors. Then we have to develop solutions that are integrated across these domains, at the same time as minimising unintended consequences.

Take, for example, the emerging evidence that access to green spaces, walkability of neighbourhoods and distribution of food outlets are all related to levels of obesity. There is no doubt, either that poor quality of the built environment, noise, fear of crime and low social cohesion are powerful influences on mental health. These place-based factors are mainly beyond the control of the individual, yet they constrain healthy life choices.

The challenge for the Welsh Government and local authorities in Wales is to create healthier places within severely limited resource constraints and with low or no economic growth. Those responsible for developing building regulations and planning of land use, housing quality, access to services and facilities, transportation, and urban renewal, are faced with difficulties of how to apply knowledge from a range of disciplines. They must design and plan for health when there are complex trade offs. Increasing opportunities for walking and cycling have the potential to reduce obesity, but will also need infrastructure adaptation to address road safety and fear of crime and to ensure accessibility to services for the elderly and disabled. Healthy housing policy must address the trade off between the benefits of warmer homes with the possibility of a more hazardous indoor air quality for asthmatics. The health challenge for schools in achieving the *One Wales One Planet* vision -the 'school run' being replaced by organised school transport or group walking or cycling - must be accompanied by measures safeguarding against increased risks of traffic injuries.

At the other end of the age spectrum the challenge is to facilitate healthy ageing and preserve independence of older people. However, autonomous living is a complex phenomenon. Loss of independence is not only related to an individual's physical and mental state but is also closely linked to mental capital, physical conditions and the supportiveness of the social and policy environments. There is a complex interplay between individual level factors, including mental capital (cognition and psychological resources), well being (human flourishing and capability) and physical ability (strength, mobility and medical conditions), and contextual factors at the micro-level (housing type, land use mix and social quality of neighbourhoods) and the meso-level (urban form, road and street networks, social networks, walkability, retail space density).

Neglected children

The Brundtland definition of sustainable development is "to meet the needs of the present generation without compromising the ability of future generations to meet their own needs". The focus is on our generation first. It speaks of future generations as if they were separate and autonomous. They are not since the next generation is already here - our children and grandchildren. The importance of our children is often inadequately articulated in discussion of sustainable development policies in the UK. This is not the case in other countries such as Sweden. As the 2005 Swedish strategy for sustainable development states:

> "Insecurity, ill health and disease at a young age often reappear at various stages later in life... Children from households that are at risk of poverty face a greater likelihood of suffering ill health or dying earlier in life than others. Improving conditions for the most economically and socially segregated districts of metropolitan areas to grow and develop is vital in that connection...For children and young people to enjoy good health, they must be provided with a decent environment both in and outside the home, at preschools, childcare facilities, elementary schools and recreation centres. In addition, they must be introduced to healthy lifestyles and be given the opportunity to grow and develop normally... Another urgent challenge is to make it easier for children to have nourishing relationships with their parents, as well as with adults and other children in school and recreation... Children and young people must also be given expanded opportunities for acquiring skills and contributing to cultural life on equal terms."

In Wales the definition of sustainable development specifically embraces responsibility for children, or 'future generations': "...sustainable development means enhancing the economic, social and environmental wellbeing of people and communities, achieving a better quality of life for our own and future generations". Rhodri Morgan put this better when he was First Minister:

> "I want a Wales fit for generations to come... What motivates me is doing my very best to ensure a brighter, sustainable future for [my grandchildren and their grandchildren] and every other child growing up in Wales today... [Therefore], top of the list... of our priorities which will continue to improve the quality of life for people today and in the future ... is sustainability."[4]

To sustain flourishing communities, public policy and public health actions must give greater priority to the generational effects of social and biological patterning of prenatal and early years risk factors. Because of the profound influence of prenatal conditions on the life course of individuals, by the time of birth many infants already have built in biological disadvantage. As the Marmot Review put it in 2010:

> "When human foetuses have to adapt to a limited supply of nutrients, they permanently change their structure and metabolism. These 'programmed' changes may be the origins of a number of diseases in later life, including coronary heart disease and the related disorders of stroke, diabetes and hypertension. Low birth weight in particular is associated with poorer long-term health outcomes and the evidence also suggests that maternal health is related to socioeconomic status. In particular, disadvantaged mothers are more likely to have babies of low birth weight."[5]

In addition, it is now absolutely clear that the formative experiences of the first few years of life have profound implications for the sustainability of society. As the Marmot review also stated:

> "What a child experiences during the early years lays down a foundation for the whole of their life. A child's physical, social, and cognitive development during the early years strongly influences their school-readiness and educational attainment, economic participation and health."

Yet the indications are that the mental health and well-being of our children is in serious trouble. A recent policy report by the UK Faculty of Public Health states that,

"Recent trend data strongly suggests that children's mental health is deteriorating with increasing prevalence of mental disorders. Early intervention is crucial to good outcomes... One in 10 children and young people suffer from a diagnosable mental disorder. Our children need a better start in life. It would be good for them, good for their life chances as well as good for society at large. This is an investment for all of us in building a stronger, healthier future, so why then is there so little investment in the early years of childhood and tackling mental health issues early? How do we build that stronger wellbeing in this country? A good start enhances children's mental, social and emotional development as well as their educational achievements. It matters because it is good for children, but also because it makes them resilient to mental and physical illness through their lives... economists throughout the world agree that investing in early childhood saves a great deal of expenditure later in life, far more than investing in the school years. And, of course, people with good mental wellbeing are those who are more likely to work and be active members of society, sharing their wellbeing with others."[6]

It is not enough, therefore, to accept that we must conserve material resources for future generations without also accepting that our individual behavior and the social and physical environments we create are themselves health resources that should not be denied our children. As the Allen report on early intervention argued in 2011:

"The recent increase in early years provision has not yet improved outcomes. The well-being of children in the UK continues to lag well behind that in other rich nations... Early intervention, while growing, is small-scale. It is often dependent on ad hoc spending and not sustained by being part of mainstream funding, and it is usually poorly evaluated."[7]

From the public health perspective there is a timely convergence of agendas across the policy spectrum. The need for a new focus on prevention of ill health and health inequalities and the growing crisis in early years mental health can only be adequately addressed within a framework that deals with the wider influences on an individual's health. This is the same framework that should tackle child poverty, poor housing, social cohesion and worklessness.

As a central organising principle the sustainable development paradigm fits the bill. But the holistic view is difficult to sustain and early intervention programmes require sustained long-term funding, well beyond the timetables of individual governments.

There will necessarily be interactions and trade offs within and between domains of economic, social and physical environments that will present difficult challenges.

The centrifugal force to pull us back to single issue concerns may be irresistible. This is the case for legislation to require Welsh Governments and local authorities to work within a sustainable development framework. This should be one that recognises the three pillars of sustainability, not just environmental protection.

Certainly there is an overwhelmingly case from a public health perspective that the Welsh Government should be required by statute to measure and monitor progress on sustainable development. The urgent need is for this to include the neglected topic of early years health and children's mental and social wellbeing. This should be an even greater priority than the current dominating concern with the here and now problems of an ageing generation and its burden on NHS resources.

Notes

1   Welsh Government Chief Medical Officer, *Annual Report*, 2010.

2   Barton, H. and Grant, M., 'A health map for the local human habitat', *Journal of the Royal Society for the Promotion of Public Health*, 126 (6) pp252-261, 2006.

3   *Securing the Future*, The UK Government's Sustainable Development Strategy, Cm 6467, 2005.

4   Rhodri Morgan, *One Wales, One Planet*, 8 February 2008.

5   Marmot Review, *Fair Society, Healthy Lives*, 2010.

6   Faculty of Public Health, *Thinking Ahead, Why we need to improve children's mental health and wellbeing*, 2011.

7   Allen report, *Early Intervention – the next steps*, 2011.

Chapter 8
Sustainable development within the European Union
Susan Baker and Katarina Eckerberg

While continuing to reply upon state interventions, contemporary governance increasingly use 'softer' approaches, such as policy networks and civil society participation.[1] This change arises in part from the pressures of globalisation and Europeanisation, but also reflects the influence of neo-liberal ideologies that emphasise the inherent inefficiencies of 'big government'. The overall result is that the state must negotiate policy and its implementation with partners across multiple levels in the public, private and voluntary sectors.

The development of network governance focuses attention on the exercise of power and the play of politics as public and private actors, at various levels, negotiate over policy. Some evidence is presented here on how the state manages these networks and the consequences for the pursuit of sustainable development.

Some argue that the promotion of sustainable development is best undertaken through the enhancement of participatory democracy.[2] It is claimed that participation leads to better policy decisions and improved implementation prospects, lending greater legitimacy to policy. On the other hand, others argue that participatory practices are weak in terms of traditional political accountability and representation.[3]

In these discussions considerable attention has been given to the notion of 'social capital'. This describes those features of society, particularly at the community level, that facilitate collective action in pursuit of sustainable development. Social capital refers to networks, shared norms, values and understandings that facilitate co-operation within and between groups.[4] Local Agenda 21 has addressed the need, particularly within rural communities, to foster the accumulation of social capital. At times, the actions of the state can improve 'social capital' for sustainable development, particularly at the local level. On other occasions, states prove to be less interested, particularly when priority is given to traditional policy goals, centred on more narrowly conceived notions of economic growth.

Governance can also occur through market-based forms of resource allocation. The use of market-based instruments has grown steadily since the early 1970s, and they now extend from subsidies through to emission charges and tradeable permits. Their use within the environmental policy arena has been extensively studied.[5] The development of less bureaucratic, more flexible, 'soft' policy instruments is seen as a key feature of contemporary governance. Despite their growing importance, we need to be mindful that the use of market instruments does not replace the regulatory approach, but are combined with hierarchical interventions. It is often argued that harnessing market forces for environmental governance helps the state to cope with the growing complexity of environmental policy, against a background of limited state institutional and administrative capacity. Whether and to what extent our evidence supports this view forms a main theme in our empirical presentation.

These four themes are the subject of this chapter: multi-level governance, networks and public/private partnerships, participation, and the use of market-based instruments.

Multi-level governance

In its role as regulator and in the formulation of strategic plans, for example the *EU Sustainable Development Strategy*, the European Union has a major influence on sustainable development policy. Strategies at the nation-state level are devised to comply with EU requirements. In turn, these function as a co-ordination tool for sub-national policy developments. The central state uses guidance on local actions plans, financial support and training programmes as a means of co-ordination.

However, central governments face a difficult task when trying to secure commitment from the sub-national levels, which often lack the capacity to act. Furthermore, while discussions of multi-level governance often assume that lower levels of government are executing policies within wider nation-state frameworks, evidence from Spain suggests that the central government has still not taken any significant action to encourage, stimulate or guide regional and local action in pursuit of sustainable development. Within Spain many sub-national levels of government have taken on this task alone. Similarly, in Germany, the Länder often become most active in areas when the federal government has failed to act.

Of course, the relationship between the different tiers of government varies across the EU member states. In some countries there is considerable decentralisation of powers (Spain and the UK), while in others centralised policy making still prevails (Ireland). Meanwhile, those with federal government systems exercise great policy autonomy and financial independence at regional level (Austria, Germany). The greater the degree of autonomy, the easier it is for locally specific needs and interests to be taken into account and for sub-national authorities to operate channels for communication and policy transfer directly with the EU level. Participatory governance processes and more substantive achievements in relation to sustainable development are chiefly found among local governments that have a high level of fiscal, legal and political autonomy.

The German case provides the most obvious example of the need to take account of constitutional arrangements. In Germany, the role of local authorities can vary, including from programme to programme, as does the extent of involvement of private sector actors. In contrast, the Irish case is illustrative of a highly centralised administrative system that continues to obstruct action at the sub-national level.

However, even in Ireland, long recognised as one of the most centralised states in the EU, there is growing emphasis on the role of regional authorities in promoting partnerships and in identifying their own regional sustainable development priorities. There is also evidence that in the Netherlands, despite the strong engagement of the local level in implementing *nationally defined* sustainable development strategies, it is increasingly working independently in promoting locally relevant strategies.

There is a distinction between multi-level governance, which refers to steering and public management, and multi-level politics, which is the distribution of power across the different levels of government. The study of policy making for sustainable development has to consider how the power relations between actors shape these processes. Indeed, one study of rural sustainable development networks in Norway, shows how this play of power is a key determinant shaping the outcomes of governance processes.[6]

There is also evidence that sustainable development becomes interpreted through existing structures and long established procedures. This underlines the importance of the institutional framework in which policies are prepared, developed and implemented. Furthermore, while the EU has helped to increase capacities at the regional level, this must not be seen as leading necessarily to enhance the pursuit of sustainable development. Other strategies, such as national development or spatial plans, often exercise a dominant influence when compared with sustainable development strategies.

They can also be tensions between different EU programmes. For example, the EU Structural Funds are more concerned with traditional economic development and, more recently, social cohesion, rather than sustainable development. In both Ireland and France the pursuit of sustainable development at the regional level is only weakly linked to sustainable development requirements. The National Development Plan in Ireland and local political interests in France prioritise economic goals before sustainable development.

In some cases, and contrary to the general trend, Europeanisation can support hierarchical governance. One study of the impact of Local Agenda 21 among the German federal states, found that Länder competences have been restricted rather than extended by European integration.[7] Compliance with EU environmental regulation can give central government a strong role, especially through centralised institutions such as the environmental protection agencies. Indeed, the need for regulatory compliance can distort the use of market and network governance arrangements at the sub-national level.

However, where network arrangements are strong, they can support innovative approaches. Towns and cities that are consistently high in sustainable development achievements are those that have worked within European networks which become conduits for the transfer of best practice. Although not a member of the EU, Norway exploits European networks to share experiences and knowledge on rural sustainable development. Similar patterns of policy transfer have been seen in Germany.

This reveals how policy transfer and benchmarking, particularly at the sub-national levels, has become important for effective governance. At the same time there can be tensions between using past learning to standardise best practice, and avoiding 'lock in' to outmoded routines. This problem has arisen in the UK, where the desire for public/private partnerships to build upon *past* success often works against the adoption of *new* initiatives and innovate approaches.

Networks and public/private partnerships

All the countries showed evidence of enhanced co-operation between the private and public sectors in support of sustainable development. This co-operation includes the engagement of interest groups in policy formulation and the construction of public/private partnerships for programme delivery. In Norway this provided new opportunities for local politicians and private stakeholders to take shared responsibility for sustainable rural development.

However, experience has shown that networks can be subject to government control from above. In some instances, government has initiated networks and shaped their frames of reference and membership. In Norway only a minor consultation role is given to sub-national networks for rural sustainable development and only rarely are they involved in exchange and negotiation based on mutual trust. Furthermore, government actors made use of their privileged position to promote their own interests within these networks, enhancing traditional hierarchical patterns of governance.[8]

In general, the provision of grants and subsidies can strengthen the hand of central government in steering the engagement of networks in governance processes, particularly in Sweden, Germany and the UK. Similarly, the Irish study indicated that hierarchical steering from central government remains an integral feature of policy processes that make use of networks. There is a danger, too, of underestimating the role that local governments continue to play in innovating, supporting and nurturing sustainable development planning and policy processes.

The case of waste management in Ireland illustrates the difficulties of relating methods and practices of participatory governance to the existing structures and processes of government. In Ireland, growing dependence on the private sector has reduced the strategic control that local authorities exercise over waste management.[9] Tensions also exist between partnership arrangements and traditional practices of representative democratic. New governance arrangements can create ambiguity and uncertainty in the eyes of both policy makers and the public about who is responsible and accountable for policy. The Irish case also directed attention to the need to explore the underlying rationale for partnership arrangements. In practice, these arrangements are often driven by new public management principles and not necessarily by the pursuit of sustainable development.

The neo-liberal belief in the power of the market was a particularly important driver in the UK. For example, while acting as a key source of funding for local sustainable development initiatives, the Lottery Fund nevertheless prioritises public-private partnerships aimed at efficiency in policy delivery, often to the detriment of wider social and ecological aims.

Participation

A key characteristic of contemporary governance is that it affords increased opportunities for citizens to have a more direct input in the making of public policy. Such participation can strengthen the legitimacy of public sector institutions. The Dutch policy of political renewal provides an excellent example of this trend.[10]

However, our evidence suggests that participatory processes are not without problems. For example, while there are several well established Dutch approaches to stakeholder engagement, participation has often occurred too late in the decision making process to allow groups to exert influence over policy decisions. There can also be a wider reluctance among public policy makers to open up the policy processes to extensive civil society participation.[11]

Effective governing for sustainable development is most likely to occur when governments work closely with civil society. This allows a strong relationship to form between people with an interest in local sustainable development issues. Nevertheless, while the study of the UK lottery funds also revealed that local authorities tend to rely upon a limited number of groups, the extent to which these were orientated towards the pursuit of sustainable development remains in doubt. In Ireland NGOs that present radical views, for example by proposing 'zero waste' strategies, remain on the fringes, with fewer opportunities to influence the agenda or policy outcomes. The Norwegian case also exposed similar problems. Here participation practices tended to be driven by emphasis on problem-solving capacity rather than on principles of stakeholder participation. Additionally, local councils tend to put the interests of their local constituency above the will to deliberate and negotiate.

These findings point to difficulties in combining representative democratic government with network governance. Yet, there is ample evidence to point to the reciprocal benefits arising from strong relationships between local government and civil society organisations, for both social cohesion and the pursuit of sustainable development.

Market based instruments

Market based instruments were found to be in use in all the countries studied. However, it proved difficult to maintain a sharp distinction between new and old policy tools. The so-called 'old' tools (for example, financial instruments) were often used not just for the purposes of hierarchical steering but also to promote network governance. Furthermore many of the market-based instruments, including voluntary agreements and public/private partnerships, required strong state engagement to kick-start and oversee their progress. The 'catalysing effect' of economic instruments was also found to work best where government efforts are linked to *existing* activities, such as Local Agenda 21.

Evidence also suggests that some tools could lead to unintended consequences for governance processes. For example, governments often use competitive procedures for the allocation of funds. This can lead to self-interested behaviour among partnerships, which can threaten to destroy the basis of future sustainable development partnerships.

Funding allocation also tends to favour quantifiable measures over more qualitative issues inherent in sustainable development. The Irish case proved particularly revealing, in that the use of public/private partnerships for the management of waste has diminished local authority control over the strategic management of waste. In addition, privatisation has led to an increase of illegal dumping in Ireland. Commercialisation turns waste into a profitable commodity, but does little to encourage waste reduction. These examples show how the use of market-based instruments may not necessarily be good for the promotion of sustainable development.

Conclusion

The state has an important role in the governance of sustainable development. It is a key player in initiating and co-ordinating sustainable development planning processes. Government plays a key role through its formal exercise of power, which sees it establishing framework legislation, developing strategies, initiating funding mechanisms, and spurring the sub-national level to engage in appropriate policies.

In short, the governance of sustainable development at the sub-national levels is still highly dependent on traditional national and supranational government structures, processes and policy priorities. National legislation and policy priorities remain key drivers for sustainable development, as are central government steering mechanisms and instruments. In addition, the state has been seen to both initiate and co-ordinate policy networks and to retain a great deal of power over the nature and functioning of network governance. Evidence also points out how the use of new environmental policy tools can strengthen the hand of the state by supporting hierarchical governance.

As to the questions of whether contemporary forms of governance help to promote a coherent approach to sustainable development, we are less certain in our verdict since the empirical research points both to competing policy goals and to frequent inconsistency between declaratory level-commitments and actual policy measures for sustainable development. We have not yet arrived at the stage where sustainable development has displaced conventional economic priorities and where the pursuit of sustainable development has become normal.

Notes

1   This chapter draws upon research undertaken together with a dozen European colleagues examining processes of planning, funding and implementing sustainable development at the sub-national level in EU member states and in Norway and published as *In Pursuit of Sustainable Development: New governance practices at the sub-national level in Europe*, Routledge, 2008.

2   Dryzek, J., *The Politics of the Earth*, Oxford University Press, 2005.

3   Hallstrom, L. K., 'Eurocratising Enlargement? EU Elites and NGO Participation in European Environmental Policy', *Environmental Politics*, 13, 1: 175-193, 2004.

4   Putnam, R. D. Ed., *Democracies in Flux: The Evolution of Social Capital in Contemporary Society*, Oxford University Press, 2004.

5   For an overview see Jordan, A., Wurzel, R. and Zito, A., Eds., *New Instruments of Environmental Governance? National Experiences and Prospects*, London: Frank Cass, 2003.

6   Hovik, S., 'Governance Networks Promoting Rural Sustainable Development in Norway', in Susan Baker S., and Eckerberg K. (Eds.), *In Pursuit of Sustainable Development: New governance practices at the sub-national level in Europe*, Routledge, 169-189, 2008.

7   Kern, K., 'Sub-National Sustainable Development Initiatives in Federal States in Germany', in Baker S. and Eckerberg K. (Eds.), *In Pursuit of Sustainable Development: New governance practices at the sub-national level in Europe*, edited by Routledge, 122-144, 2008.

8   Hovik, *op.cit.*

9   Connaughton, B., Quinn, B. and Rees, N., 'Rhetoric or Reality: Responding to the challenge of sustainable development and new governance patterns in Ireland', in Baker S. and Eckerberg K. (Eds.), *In Pursuit of Sustainable Development: New governance practices at the sub-national level in Europe*, Routledge, 2008.

10   Coenen, F., 'New Interpretations of Local Governance for Sustainable Development in the Netherlands', in Baker S. and Eckerberg K. (Eds.), *In Pursuit of Sustainable Development: New governance practices at the sub-national level in Europe*, Routledge, 190-207, 2008.

11   Hovik, *op.cit.*

Chapter 9
The Hungarian experience
Sándor Fülöp

Hungary had an independent parliamentary ombudsman office between 2008 and 2011. From 2012, this was transformed into a deputy position with strong legitimacy and still wide enough rights and responsibilities. In the following article we survey the work and results of the independent office and try to deduct some general conclusions.

Institutional guarantees of sustainable development
Sustainable development goals are easy to acknowledge, but difficult to apply in every day social and economic life. In several countries, politicians and journalists frequently claim to have excellent sustainable development plans and environmental laws, while there are still some shortcomings and incomplete measures in implementation. Environmental legislation or a plan for sustainable development cannot be good if it allows for faulty implementation. There are certain legal techniques and institutional solutions through which a much higher success rate could be achieved in implementation.

The short history of environmental law is rich in creative ideas serving the more effective prevention of environmental pollution and the introduction of proactive, longer-term approaches into decision-making procedures. In many countries, for instance, we see environmental impact assessments, a flagship of modern environmental law. Generally there is a whole family of laws related to impact assessment, for

- Strategies and legislation.
- Plans, policies and programs.
- Future, individual projects.
- Ongoing projects - partly monitoring the effects of earlier assessments, partly as sanctions or precautionary measures.
- Large international projects.
- Smaller local activities - starting out from the consideration that the environmental effects of such SMEs could add up to serious environmental problems.
- Certain fields of administration closely related to environmental protection, for

instance specific assessments for large energy investments, Natura 2000 sites or cultural heritage.

A key to the effectiveness of an Environment Impact Assessment is its internal rules. To what extent is the multidisciplinary approach achieved in the procedure? How independent are the experts preparing the several sections of the environmental impact study? How widely and deeply can the concerned public and the environmental NGOs participate in the procedure (especially important are the viewpoints of early and informed participation)? And how much support do the environmental authorities receive in decision-making?

Externally, the decisive factors are the legal effects of an Environment Impact Assessment decision and the extent to which it becomes embedded into the flow of the licensing and monitoring procedures of large investments. If spatial planning bodies or construction-permitting authorities can simply overlook the documents, even well designed and carefully implemented Assessment procedures could all be in vain.

Environment Impact Assessment is only one example of the creative solutions of modern environmental laws. We could also refer to the principles and their legal effects - such as the integration principle, the precautionary principle and the polluter pays principle - that bring new approaches into the tissue of our legal systems. Regulation of public participation is also a revolutionary legal tool that raises the level of governance in environmental protection matters. Such innovative legal solutions are nowadays added by the creation of specific state environmental institutions that are independent from the executive power. Their primary task is to ensure that the system of environmental law, and laws serving sustainable development more generally, are used in a consequential and more effective manner.

International examples of creative sustainable development institutions

Some countries that have already introduced state level institutions whose primary responsibility is to monitor and support sustainable development. The first modern was New Zealand's Environmental Commissioner, who was first elected in 1987 for seven years. Since then several commissioners have held the office with great success and social acknowledgement. The New Zealand Commissioner does not deal with individual cases, but organises wide ranging social discussions about vital social and environmental problems, such as sustainable agriculture, and issues in-depth analyses and suggestions.

Between 1990 and 1994, an Environmental Chief Prosecutor operated in New Jersey, a popular and effective institution. His office had the same rank as the general attorney's and had direct access to the state and county level administrative systems, although it was not directly a part of the government. While the environmental prosecutor was mainly active in individual administrative, civil and criminal enforcement cases, he also dealt with structural issues, like raising the sensitivity of the law enforcement units toward environmental matters, including the marine police and road patrols.

In the early 2000s the Israeli Knesset elected a Parliamentary Commission for Future Generations, with strong legislative advocacy roles. They could halt any law-drafting procedure if they found it was not in harmony with long-term environmental interests. A similar parliamentary commission operates in Finland. In Hungary, between 2008 and 2011, we had an ombudsman for future generations. Countries that might introduce similar institutions in the near future include Wales, Malta and Belgium. In Austria and Canada, an environmental ombudsman works within the governmental system, but with considerable independence in administrative and budgetary aspects.

A survey of these sustainable development institutions shows that they have three functions, or some combination of these: complaint handling, legislative advocacy, and think tank type activities. Out of these three, the specific institutions put stress on different ones in different combinations.

The potential for a global sustainable development institution

The secretariat of the Rio+20 conference has prepared the initial draft of the outcome document. Paragraph 57 addresses the problem of institutional representation of future generations:

> "We agree to further consider the establishment of an Ombudsperson, or High Commissioner for Future Generations, to promote sustainable development".

Several other documents, including those issued by the majority of the Stakeholder Forum members, and also the conference declaration of the European Economic and Social Council in February 2012, refer to the necessity of such institutional solutions that could counterbalance the short-term way of thinking of governments and major economic actors.

A global level ombudsman for Future Generations or High Commissioner for Sustainable Development would have a real chance of addressing the challenges of implementing sustainable development policies. It is most likely that this person would have responsibility for performing the same three main tasks that confront national Sustainable Development Commissioners. Apart from this, the mere existence of such an UN-level institution would support the network of the already existing sustainable development institutions. The possibility that a complaint could reach this global institution would send serious messages to the national level authorities. It would be a tremendous help for the national environmental administrative bodies and other organisations aiming for the protection of future generations' interests. This way the national level authorities might be considered as procedural filters that prevent the given country from getting into conflict with generally accepted international norms and values of protecting the interests of future generations.

Establishing the Hungarian Future Generations Ombudsman

Environmental protection played a special role in changing the political regime in Hungary. In the early 1990s nearly every decision-maker was enthusiastic about developing ambitious environmental laws and institutions. During these early years, an ombudsman for environmental matters was agreed and even the first draft of the General Environmental Code had a clear reference to it. However, as time passed by, the enthusiasm tapered down.

Many scholars, especially the ombudspersons already in charge, claimed that this new ombudsman position would lead to 'ombudsman inflation', that is the growing number of ombudspersons would decrease the level of their prestige. Our view was that if all the suppressed social interests receive high level, independent institutional protection they would not diminish, but rather mutually reinforce each other's effectiveness and social appreciation. However, institutionalisation is not an arbitrary decision, but rather an organic development. Whenever a social issue produces a critical mass of conflicts it attracts many supporters, and when other social and financial conditions gradually get together it will have its institutions sooner or later.

In the case of the Hungarian Ombudsman for Future Generations this time arrived at the end of an almost decade-long fight as well as coalition-building and patience from the NGO 'Védegylet' (Protect the Future). They could complete a five-party agreement about the modification of the Ombudsman Act in 2007, and the inclusion of the rules about the new ombudsman institution.

However, by the time of the election of the ombudsman for future generations in 2008 there was no party agreement – or, rather, a concerted disagreement of the parliamentary parties. The president of Hungary wanted to achieve the fullest possible independence for the new official and therefore did not run the usual informal negotiations with the parties about the person whom he would nominate. In turn, the parties failed to give their votes to the presidential nominees in three consecutive voting rounds. Finally, the consequential efforts from the president prevailed and the fourth nominee got the required two-third majority.

Design of the Hungarian Ombudsman for Future Generations

The new Hungarian ombudsman had all the three basic functions mentioned above: handling complaints, running legislative advocacy activities, and performing think-tank functions. He had the right to receive complaints from citizens and organisations where the regular legal remedies were exhausted but the court remedies were not yet used.

Apart from the up to 300 substantial complaints a year, the ombudsman himself has initiated a few dozen cases *ex officio*, based on information from the press, professionals or NGOs. In addition to these, if we learnt from the mass of complaints, that certain fields of environmental enforcement were especially crowded with system faults, we started overall, systematic investigations. Examples of such general examinations were in relation to city noise (caused by roads, pubs, open space public events), and urban sprawl (loss of the last green spaces in and around bigger cities). We undertook file research in the archives of the authorities concerned, structured interviews with officials, literature analyses, as well as conferences summarising and discussing the results. These concluded with an official statement with a series of legislative and practical proposals to the governmental bodies affected.

As concerns legislative advocacy, Ombudsman representatives were present in the relevant Parliamentary Commissions. We also regularly scanned the legislative plans and drafts of several ministries in order to find any proposals in conflict with the interests of future generations. In dozens of cases, such as the Forestry Act, the Danube Plan, the genetic heritage of the country, and the use of underground waters we successfully influenced the legislative procedures in close alliance with the relevant scientific and civil organisations and experts.

Finally, within the frames of the think-tank activity, during its five years of existence the Ombudsman initiated general research and social discussion topics. These included sustainable local communities, alternative indicators, environmental education and the rights of future generations in the Constitution. We organised several national and international conferences, supported and took part in research activities and networking with stakeholders and issued legislative and practical proposals to the government and other relevant organisations.

The responsibilities and rights of the Future Generations Ombudsman were listed in the Ombudsman Act on two levels:

1. He was obliged to be a guardian of the environmental protection interests of present and future generations.
2. He was provided with a list of specific measures the Ombudsman could use to achieve these general tasks.

The legal tools guaranteed almost unlimited access to any state and private documents. An expedited procedure at the Budapest City Court was at our disposal in case the targeted persons hesitated to issue the documents or information required – although we never had to use this legal tool. We also had the right to ask for professional help from any institution or expert.

Apart from the rights and responsibility to examine administrative files and establish constitutional irregularities, or system faults, the Ombudsman had the right to start administrative and civil court cases against authorities or private persons. He could also step into court procedures initiated by others as *amicus curae*. Based on the old wisdom that environmental pollution does not stop at the borders, the Ombudsman also had strong international responsibilities, including participation in forming and implementing Hungary's international environmental policies. Naturally, such an exceptionally strong mandate could not be performed without the support of the Ministry of Foreign Affairs.

We tried to design the structure of the office according to these tasks. The personnel of 34 were divided between lawyers and environmental policy experts, including biologists, chemists, environmental engineers, and environmental economists. We also had an international environmental legal unit and a small organisational or coordination unit, although the general supporting services were performed mostly by the joint office of the four ombudspersons at that time.

Naturally, such a wide range of responsibility could not have been performed with such a small staff alone. The Ombudsman invested a lot of time in developing a wide network of NGOs, churches, professional bodies, experts of several administrative bodies and others. Our methodology was in harmony with these networking efforts. In every important case and legislative matter, we followed a deliberative, iterative procedure with a wide range of consultations on conceptual papers and draft statements. Only in this way could we hope that our otherwise non-binding statements would substantially influence the legislation and practice of environmental law in the country.

Impact of the Hungarian Future Generations Ombudsman

Without the Future Generations Ombudsman:

- A large power plant would have been established in one of the most valuable nature and history world heritage site of Hungary, the Tokaj vineyard region;
- There would be a military radio locator built just above Pécs, exposing the city of 160,000 to unprecedented short wave radiation.
- One of the last major green spots around Budapest would have disappeared, including the large fruit tree genetic sample collection of Érd city.
- Numerous communities would still suffer from noise of constructions, roads, pubs and open space festivals;
- Large technical sport events such as the Hungarian Dakar Rally and the Red Bull Air Race could use valuable nature protection and historical sites undisturbed and without paying attention to the consequences.
- The Forestry Act would provide much less protection for valuable natural forests and fewer opportunities for public participation.
- The Water Utilities Plan would have resulted in a reorganisation without due consideration of the environmental aspects and the safest service viewpoints.
- The regulation of Danube and Tisza rivers would have been continued without due respect to all the ecological services concerned.
- The General Administrative Act would have guaranteed far fewer rights for civic organisations; and many other laws would have overlooked the environmental protection interests of present and future generations.

As concerns the third ombudsman function, the think-tank activity, the Ombudsman organised or co-ordinated:

- A strong sustainable local communities project, including programmes to ensure

access to local markets for healthy local agricultural products.
- Green public procurement.
- Several actions for saving the country's rich agricultural genetic heritage.
- The legal possibilities of using alternative, ecological building materials.
- Cultivating the ancient practices of herb culture.

The results of our sustainable local communities project were solidified in September 2011 by the Pannonhalma Declaration at a conference held in the oldest monastery of Hungary with more than 100 top level administrative and scientific experts. At the same time, the Ombudsman, eight bishops, two archbishops, the leaders of the Ministry responsible for agriculture and environment, and a number of civic and scientific experts signed a Memorandum of Understanding about saving and nurturing ancient fruit trees in church gardens. Since then, we have started to work with more than 70 church gardens and with agricultural engineers to plant old species suited to the particular landscapes and offering community activity to carry on the old customs connected to these fruits. Also within the frames of the think-tank function, the Ombudsman has run a project on alternative social-environmental indicators, and another initiative on greening the budget.

The general mandate of future generation institutions

The staff of the Hungarian Future Generations Ombudsman delivered more than 150 conference lectures a year, mostly on national issues but also at the international level. Apart from intensive networking in Hungary, we took part in such important international networks as the Balaton Group of lead environmental scientists and the World Future Council. As a result of these contacts our own idea about the role of the Ombudsman evolved.

We believe that bodies such as the Hungarian Future Generations Ombudsman have a responsibility to bridge the messages from science to society about planetary boundaries, resilience and intergenerational justice. We must work on clarifying the consequences of our present social and economic practices. Society tends to deceive itself. We see more and more clearly the results of climate change, biodiversity loss, arable land eradication - the three areas in which humankind has exceeded the so-called tipping points - and many other features, such as chemical safety, land and sea waste management problems, the ozone hole and so on. Even so, people are continuing and even accelerating their harmful social and economic practices. Some institutions need to keep this discrepancy at the forefront of public attention.

Our societies desperately need to be encouraged to undertake mitigation activities and resilience planning. The minimum requirement is to prevent decisions that harm the environment and the interests of future generations. Really loud and unambiguous messages need to be sent on these matters.

The life and work of Future Generations institutions are not easy. We are familiar with the old medieval practice of killing the messengers, whenever they bring bad news. This phenomenon is well known in the modern age as well. So whilst the ombudspersons, commissioners and other similar institutions are fighting against harmful social and economic attitudes, policies and deeds, they have to be aware that they themselves are very much an endangered species. Wide national and international networking are of help, but they not always enough to save the life of our institutions.

Key requirements for future generation institutions
Nonetheless, it is pleasing that more institutions for future generations are being established worldwide than are endangered with extinction. It is therefore worth summarising briefly what should be the key operational requirements institutions for future generations:

1. **Independence** from the government and from any strong social and economic interest is the major factor in the effective work of future generations' institutions. Independence allows them to reveal and evaluate the facts of their cases properly, and it also provides their prestige. It is undermined if a governmental body has significant influence on the budget, personnel policy, case selection, client policies or decisions of such bodies.

2. **Informal power** Future Generation institutions need as much informal power as possible since, because they are not part of the governmental system, they cannot bring any binding decisions in administrative cases. It is a paradox that formal power - for example, issuing legal injunctions - might even decrease the social prestige of the ombudsman, because the institution is more likely to be seen as 'part of the system'.

3. **Full access to the files** Some level of official power is indispensable for Future Generation institutions. They must have access to information and data that authorities and even private persons hold. This is the basis of the statements of ombudspersons in individual cases and in those connected with plans, policies or legislation.

4. **Exceptional official powers** In some cases access to courts, especially to those dealing with the supervision of administrative decisions, might be beneficial. As we have seen in the Hungarian case, rights to interfere with international matters can be helpful as well, but this is highly dependent on the co-operation of the professional Foreign Service.

5. **Parliamentary support** It is beyond question that the best constituency of the parliamentary commissioner for future generations is the Parliament itself. It is really important that the Parliament and other institutions connected to the Government, such as local authorities, environmental bodies, agriculture and forestry organisations, share in the ownership of the Future Generation institution and support it wholeheartedly. It is advisable that the Ombudsman meets regularly with members of the relevant Parliamentary committees to share information.

6. **Networking** Without a strong scientific and social network nationally and internationally, Ombudsman for Future Generations would be paralysed. A priority is to maintain close relations with environmental organisations at a grassroots level and to be open at all times to their feedback.

7. **Good staff** Without high quality, multidisciplinary staff the Ombudsman for Future Generations is just a faint copy of the administrative bodies.

With all these features a new kind of state organisation can emerge. It will have a high level of professional and social prestige, have a chance to stop harmful investments, and even change the social habits that infringe the environmental rights of present and future generations.

Chapter 10
Overshooting limits: seeking a new paradigm
Gareth Wyn Jones[1]

Characteristically humans espouse many and various life styles, political and economic systems, religions and philosophies. However perhaps the most far-reaching division is between those convinced that there are tangible limits to humanity's ability to extract goods and services from the planet and those who do not. Broadly speaking the latter believe that the creative and destructive powers of capitalism and free market forces, combined with scientific progress, human ingenuity and technical innovations, can circumvent all supposed limits. A few even appeal to divine intervention.

The 'optimists' argue that, just as in Edwardian London concerns about being overwhelmed by horse manure were obviated by the combustion engine, and the Liverpool smog of my youth succumbed to the Clean Air Acts, humanity can and will harness other better technologies of limitless potential. Human, horse and waterpower have been superseded by coal-fired engines, then by diesel, gas and electric motors. Now we have miniaturized electronics and nano-technology. Our technical prowess is astounding. Mobile cell phones, helicopters and aircraft have transformed communications even in the remotest corners of this planet.

Even the nuclear holocaust so feared in the 1950s and 1960s has been avoided. Indeed, communism itself appears to have been vanquished. Fewer children now die in infancy but Malthus has not been vindicated. A significant and increasing proportion of this planet's 7 billion human inhabitants are enjoying historically undreamt of prosperity. We are living longer despite HIV/Aids. In most areas food supply has comfortably kept pace with the rising population. The picture may not be 'panglossian' but is nevertheless impressive. It is claimed we can and will increase wealth, measured by global GDP, indefinitely. Indeed we may even colonise other planets. By this account, economic growth, as currently construed, is not only a good measure of success but also the vital policy objective. Those worrying about 'limits' are deemed misguided and wilfully undermining the hopes and aspirations of the poor.

Given this scenario it is surprising that many, including eminent sober scientists, remain deeply pessimistic about mankind's future and concerned at the scale of humanity's impact upon planet Earth.[2] Knowledgeable and reputable doom-mongers abound. Is this simply sour grapes, anti-capitalist propaganda or an ignorant contrarian spirit? Since pessimism about humanities' future has been rife for millennia, we must ask whether it is really different this time. Indeed, as some claim, is humankind now standing at a critical crossroad having to make, or perhaps refusing to make, decisions of epic significance? If you conclude that the free market, apparently 'optimistic' analysis is a dangerous mixture of self-deception and self-aggrandisement, often promoted by those who have appropriated to themselves a disproportionately large faction of this planet's resources, then these may be very dark and challenging times indeed. Without analysing this fundamental issue, all talk of applying 'sustainable development' in a Welsh or international context is potentially misleading, even pernicious.

Let us recognize at the outset that most of the planet's 7 billion human inhabitants are not engaged with these issues. If poor (still perhaps 80 per cent of us), they remain weighed down by immemorial problems. If relatively rich, they resent any challenge to their aspirations and achievements, especially the seductive American dream. Others are worried simply about retaining their jobs or paying off their debts. Some put their trust in an all-powerful, external God or Allah to provide providentially all the answers and resources to true believers. Any acceptance of limits, and, even more crucially, that mankind is fast approaching them, has far reaching implications. Such a conclusion must impact profoundly on our ethical, political, religious, economic and social thinking.

For centuries the older generation has perceived youth as feckless, irresponsible, and ill prepared to shoulder their responsibilities. In contrast, may not fecklessness and irresponsibility and a lack of foresight be defining traits of an older generation, my own generation? Are we handing to our children and our children's children a veritable Eden or a poisoned chalice? Many voices have been raised to warn us, others to reassure. Maybe we are instinctively aware of the dangers but are in denial. Are we too self-engrossed and too self-serving to react; too comfortable to act decisively and intelligently?

The ambiguity of affluence

> In a global free market there is variation on Gresham's law; bad capitalism tends to drive out good.
> John Gray

The possibility of a tainted inheritance is powerfully illustrated in two books, both now over 40 years old. Superficially they appear to address very different topics. Certainly, they are formulated by authors from very different traditions, rooted in contrasting disciplines. Incidentally, however, we can thank Boston, Massachusetts for both. Nevertheless, their central message is remarkably similar.

The first volume is *The Affluent Society* by the Scots-Canadian Harvard economist, John Kenneth Galbraith.[3] He was an academic patrician closely involved with the US Democratic Party and US policy for many decades, including as Kennedy's ambassador in India in the 1960s. First published in 1958 his book has enjoyed popular success and run into numerous editions over 40 years. It foresaw, with startling precision, the global financial disarray, which has gripped us since 2007-8. The second enjoys its 40th anniversary this year. The *Limits to Growth* was first published in 1972, describing work supported by the Club of Rome.[4] The initial volume by a group based at MIT led by Donella Meadows, Jorgen Randers and Dennis Meadows, has been followed by two other volumes, *Beyond the Limits* in 1992, and *Limits to Growth: the 30-year update* in 2004.[5] A further update will appear in late 2012.

Despite their popularity both books have been widely and wildly abused and misconstrued. Galbraith, as a humane political economist, welcomed the great leap in much of western capitalist society from abject poverty to affluence in a couple of centuries. All but a minuscule élite have moved from scraping a living on minimal resources which used to meet our most urgent needs - food, safe water, shelter, clothing - to widespread affluence.

By the late 1950s an impressive range of consumer goods had become available in the USA, in 'you've never had it so good' Britain and elsewhere. Now vastly more have been added. Middle class housing has improved beyond recognition; central heating and at least one car is the norm. Every home should boast a huge flat-screen television, a clothes drier, dish washer and, of course, computers, the internet and a variety of mobile phones and iPads. This affluence has spread. As the goods and services on offer have multiplied many-fold, so some hundreds of millions of Chinese, Brazilians and Indians as well as Europeans and Americans have joined the comfortable middle class.

In Galbraith's analysis, when basic human needs are satisfied, continued affluence depends on an implicit, largely unspoken, economic 'bargain' between three main parties - the general public, industrialists and business, and politicians. Each of these parties has a rational self-interest in adhering to this bargain (see Figure 1). The public, individually and collectively, wishes to retain, and, if at all possible increase, its affluence and spending power. This in turn depends on the availability of preferably well paid jobs to maintain individuals and their families and protect their buying power and social status as well as work in the public services.

Jobs require flourishing businesses and a solvent government, being derived from the provision of goods and services. To maintain this dynamic, the range and quantity of these goods and services needs to be renewed and expanded continuously through private and public innovation and investment. These innovations can range from new IT gadgets or new cars, to providing care for an ageing population or new drugs. The new affluence itself has bred new wants, from holidays in the sun, to caravans in Abersoch, gourmet foods, fine wines and the latest fashions. More recently this has been eloquently described in "the story of stuff".[6]

Realising in Clinton's famous phrase that "it's the economy stupid", politicians must oil the wheels of this 'bargain' if they are to be re-elected by a relatively contented populace. Industrialists have a strong vested interest in ensuring the continual turning of the cycle so that their businesses may prosper. To help sustain the bargain, multi-billion industries such as advertising and product promotion, as well as novel design, have grown dramatically to convince the public of its urgent need for both traditional and innovative goods and services. It has also spawned brand loyalty, celebrity endorsement and a range of more subtle psychological strategies to stoke and stimulate our desires. If demand is waning or weak, it must be created!

Entirely reasonably and logically, business has also lubricated the wheel by devices such as hire purchase, easy credit, tempting special offers, all supplemented by ubiquitous credit and debit cards and loans. In many and subtle ways people are encouraged to take on debt, especially by buying and fitting out a home fulfilling the dream of a self-reliant citizen in a property-owning democracy. Companies must themselves borrow to compete and to invest in new exciting products, services or new outlets. In turn, government must borrow to play their part in keeping the economic wheels turning by investing in education, infrastructure and dampening the business cycles so as to reduce social discontent and seek to ensure its own re-election and political survival (sometimes propping up failures to do so). Credit and debt lubricate the whole system, giving huge power to financiers who emerge as the puppet masters.

Critically the cycle must continuously turn, recorded as an annual growth in economic activity measured by Gross Domestic Product (GDP) or its derivatives. The rate varies widely from country to country. In China growth at better than 7 per cent implies a doubling of activity every decade. The UK dreams of an annual three per cent growth rate. The model is predicated on continuous exponential growth in activity. It must spin like a top and grow like Topsy to retain stability. What seemed, in the first instance, a wonderful transformation for humanity (at least the affluent minority) has become a treadmill and a never-ending grind. As Galbraith foresaw, left to its own devices, the 'bargain' to which all the parties have enthusiastically subscribed, ensures vested interests turn a blind-eye to mounting debt. He saw the system as intrinsically unstable, leading inevitably to excessive, unsustainable debt, to overshoot and painfully bursting economic bubbles. He suggested that the natural tendency to **overshoot** was caused by over-optimism, aided and abetted by 'conventional wisdom'. Moreover, the human capacity for self-delusion delayed any appreciation of reality with, of course, an added injection of greed and self-interested deceit. The system required tight control.

Figure 1: The Galbraithian bargain

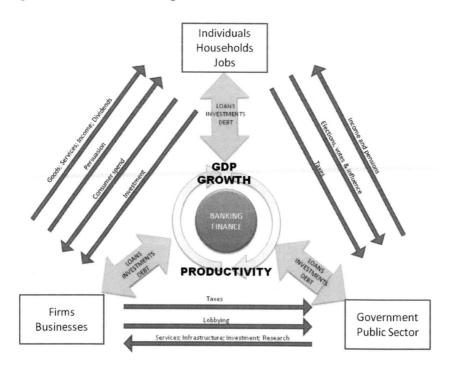

According to what I refer to as the Galbraithian bargain, affluence requires a continually and indefinitely accelerating cycle of product innovation and consumer demand, supported by government and oiled by debt. Our economic success commits us to living on an ever-accelerating treadmill.

While emphasising the need for prudent regulation and careful economic management, Galbraith also recognized a tendency to public squalor despite private plenty. He suggested that public finances would inevitably come under pressure, as power and financial clout would accrue to a small élite. Affluence could reduce civic and collective pride and commitment.

In 2012 we can conclude unambiguously that our politicians and economists should have taken Galbraith's diagnosis much more seriously. However, central to his insight was the improbability of their doing so. Ironically, even countries such as Germany, reluctant since the war to promote excessive internal spending and debt, have been trapped in the maelstrom. Although the butt of much Anglo-American criticism for their caution, they are now caught up in the whirlpool as their exports depended on demand from debt-laden markets and their banks are in hock to the debts of other countries.

Galbraith recognised that, as intermediaries and the controllers of credit, bankers wielded enormous power. However, he did not anticipate several factors. First, was the invention of clever packages which would allow risky debts to be sold on as triple A-rated financial products only tangentially related to the real world. Not only would the money market encourage the poor to take on un-repayable debts, but these would be repackaged as deceitfully desirable, highly rewarding, and apparently safe investment products. This and an array of devices, such as credit fault swaps, derivatives and the like, led to increasing instability. Secondly, both in the USA and the UK, the cult of the infallibility of the unfettered market led to deregulation, first under Reagan and Thatcher, and then Bush, Blair and Brown. Both were contrary to Galbraith's recommendations.

In the UK the 'big bang' in the city, and in the USA the repeal of the Glass-Steagall Act by the Gram-Leach-Billey Act in 1999, helped ensure 'irrational exuberance' whose most influential cheerleader was, paradoxically, the Chairman of the US Federal Reserve, Allan Greenspan himself. A few statistics will be pertinent here. In 2010 global foreign currency transactions totalled $955 trillion. Off-exchange trading in financial derivatives was $601 trillion. Meanwhile, the traded volume of shares and bonds was $78 trillion, compared with the global gross domestic product of $63 trillion. This leverage and exploitation of vast sums of 'virtual' money has allowed the emergence of hyper-rich individuals to emerge in the real world.[7]

Thirdly, and certainly in the UK, government appeared to become reliant on the financial service sector for a significant part of their tax revenues and consequently on this sector to fund many public services. The sector became untouchable, holding, and continuing to try to hold the country to ransom. This was despite Adair Turner's recognition, as chairman of the Financial Services Authority in London, that much of their activity had no public benefit. Moreover, a recent report quotes the taxes paid by the financial sector from 2002 to 2008 as £193 billion but that from manufacturing in the period as £378 billion.[8] Following the crash, direct government support to the financial sector was put at £298 billion and with loans and underwriting at £1.7 trillion. If these figures are correct, then either the City's PR apparatus is quite exceptional or other darker factors are at play. The problematical situation has been compounded by leverage buy-outs converting capital into debt, by huge global trading imbalances, and by the ability of the rich to avoid paying taxes by recourse to tax havens and to use their enormous wealth to promote disinformation and protect their narrow self-interest.

Galbraith's fears have been realized, his diagnosis confirmed. The policy makers and politicians of successive governments in many countries - Ireland, Iceland, the UK and the USA to name only but four - have been seduced by their blind faith in the infallibility of the markets. Deregulation was the war cry of Tory and Labour alike, a process abetted by a number of prominent academic economists. Now we have to account for this folly. In the UK, the tension between the desire to lower the personal and national debt burden and the fear of stoking a downward spiral of activity and employment because of a lack of demand is being played out.

The lessons of Galbraith and also of Keynes seem drowned out as countries fear the verdicts of the rating agencies and subsequent reprisals by the same financial markets which were a major cause of the collapse. It is a bitter irony that the excesses of these same markets and their analysts who helped foul up in the first place, now need placating. Finance is now in short supply and economic growth to reduce unemployment is illusive. We are living the consequences of **overshoot**.

Growth and overshoot

I don't think much of the science of the beastly scientists.
Victor Hugo

Science clears the field for technology.
Heisenberg

In large measure *The Limits to Growth* also deals with the danger of **overshoot**.[9] The initial slim volume in 1972 analysed a relatively simple model for the interdependence of population growth, industrial production, pollution, resource depletion and demand, including food production, land availability and capital demand. Central to their thinking were three factors. First, the nature of exponential growth; second, the time lags in the responses of most natural systems which lead inexorably to overshoot; and, third, the absence of a precise limit.

Meadows and her colleagues did not envisage our planetary system approaching a cliff edge, such as when the flat-earthers warned Columbus he would sail off the edge of the known world. Rather, the authors anticipated a decline, which could be gradual or rapid but would be greatly exacerbated by 'overshoot'. More and more human and natural resources would have to be directed to combating some limiting factor – be it reducing the negative impact of pollution, acquiring some scarce metal, or securing water or food supplies. In turn, this resource distortion would undermine living standards and create the potential for social disorder. I would add that this would also subvert the Galbraithian bargain, although Meadows and her colleagues did not refer to it.

Critical to their analysis was exponential growth itself, as shown in Table 1.

Table 1: Relationship of exponential growth rate to doubling time - applicable to factors such as GDP, population, and resource use.

Growth rate(% per year)	Doubling time (years)
0.5	140
1.0	70
2.0	35
3.0	23
4.0	17.5
7.0	10
10.0	7

Even a modest 2 per cent exponential growth in a factor such as population or GDP, or in demand for a valuable but rare metal or food, causes a doubling in only 35 years, about a generation. At an annual 2 per cent compound growth, our current global population of around 7 billion would theoretically, but of course improbably, reach 14 billion by 2046, and, even more improbably, 28 billion by 2080 compared with 3 billion in 1960. The equivalent UK population figures would be over 120 million in 2046 and near 250 million by 2080.

Politically an annual GDP growth of 1 per cent is regarded as lamentable, inadequate to maintain employment and rising living standards. Nevertheless, mathematically or in resource terms, it is significant. The conventional political aim is an annual GDP growth near to 3 per cent to ensure full employment, pay for pensions and public services for an aging population. But this implies a doubling every 23 years. Can this possibly be sustained? The fundamental conclusion of Meadows and colleagues was that it cannot and the current economic growth model is not sustainable.

Two major criticisms have been leveled at the *Limits to Growth*. One is that in the last 40 years we have not hit the brick wall. Indeed, on a global scale, economic growth has never been faster. More than 2 billion Indians and Chinese, or at least a skewed proportion of them, are reveling in an annual 7 to 10 per cent GDP growth. However, as noted, Meadows and her colleagues didn't foresee a precipitous sudden halt. Rather she anticipated the 'limits' gradually tightening their grip in the 21st not the 20th Century. Secondly, they were accused of underestimating human ingenuity and the dynamic power of modern technology and the market economy. This they deny.

Indeed, the latter argument has little substance. As discussed later, technological interventions are essential – the question is *which technologies?* Some low environmental-impact technologies have advanced rapidly, for example, greatly improved home insulation and waste recycling, CFC-free refrigerators, photovoltaic cells, more fuel-efficient cars. No doubt pollution of the UK's seas and fresh waters has declined. The 1987 Montreal Protocol to curb CFC emissions and allow the Polar ozone holes to recover, seems to be a success.[10] But switching technologies may bring their own resource constraints. Moving from fossil fuels to wind turbines may reduce demand for oil and gas, but increases the demand for rare earth metals for the electrical circuitry of the turbines. There are few, if any, free-meals.

If overshoot is a dreaded feature of our economic system, it is an intrinsic character of natural systems. Despite the Protocol, the ozone hole persists. Only by 2050 is it hoped that it will recover. If female fertility drops to the basic replenishment rate

(2.2 children per woman), it will take decades for population growth to decline to zero because of a pyramidal population structure – that is the presence of many fertile women in their teens and early twenties. In relation to climate change, even if anthropogenic greenhouse gas emissions, especially carbon dioxide (CO_2), were to stabilize or even to fall to pre-industrial levels tomorrow, it would take hundreds, maybe thousands of years, for the climate, oceanic circulations and sea levels to re-equilibrate (see Figure 2). Some but not all over-used aquifers could refill in time but it would take many decades, not the few years during which they exploit them. The fish stocks of Newfoundland Grand Banks have not been replenished despite a moratorium imposed some 15 years ago.[11] If we continue to cause the extinction of species then, maybe, in time new evolutionary niches will arise for new species but on a millennial not a decadal time scale.

It is interesting to address some up-to-date examples of the 'limits' dilemma and their implications. I will consider, briefly, mineral, energy and food supplies because of their global ramifications (global water shortage is equally pertinent but has less resonance in Wales). Between them they illustrate different facets of the global challenges with which we may not be sufficiently familiar.

A striking analysis of mineral supply is found the 2011 Risk List published by British Geological Survey, which assessed the supply risk of economically important chemical elements on a scale of 1 to 10.[12] The rating depended on:

• Scarcity, in terms of crystal abundance.
• Production concentrated in limited number of countries,
• Location and distribution of potentially exploitable base reserves.
• Political stability of producing countries.

On this basis, relatively little known elements such as antimony, the platinum group mercury, and tungsten receive the highest risk rating of 8.5, followed by the rare earths and niobium. These elements have become widely used in high-tech materials such as in microelectronics, catalysts, special alloys, semi-conductors and fire and temperature resistance products. At the other extreme lie the abundant and familiar elements: titanium, aluminium, chromium, iron, and sulphur.

Our advanced technologies have created new resource demands, including for materials or elements that are rare and often toxic. As some of the high supply-risk elements are essential to modern devices, securing an uninterrupted reliable supply is now a major objective of powerful nations especially China. Similarly, maintaining its gas and oil supplies has long been an American obsession, even at the expense of others. So it is apparent that the 'risk' is not simply one of geological abundance or even mining technology but the interaction between geology and economic, political and even military might. So for example, in late 2011 *Rare Earth Investment News* reported that the price of Cerium, used in energy efficient LED lights, increased from $50 to $413 per kilogram between January and June 2011 threatening the industry and leading to flight of companies to China. The limitations of market and state capitalism in accessing and allocating resources are all too apparent and fundamental problems remain unresolved.

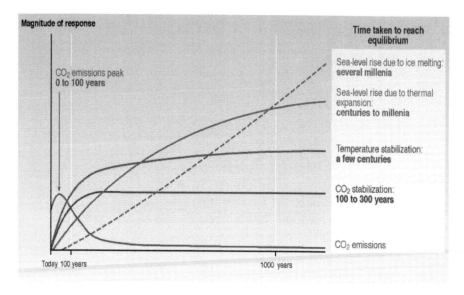

Figure 2: Lags in climate change and overshoots
Source: R.T. Watson and the Core Writing Team (eds.), *Climate Change 2001: Synthesis Report. A Contribution of Working Groups I, II, and III to the Third Assessment Report of the Intergovernmental Panel on Climate Change*, Cambridge University Press, Cambridge 2001.

Figures 3a and 3b illustrate the near exponential growth and price fluctuations in world copper production. These reflect the impact of global economic growth and futures speculation as well as possibly the feedback effects of demand and supply scarcity on the market price. In the wake of the 2008 crash the price fell back but has now been on rising trajectory for about 6 months, to ~$8,500 per tonnes. Again major companies and nations are hell-bent on securing a dominant market share of this resource.

Another even more challenging, but dauntingly complex, aspect of 'limits' is illustrated by the web of food supply, land availability, water for irrigation and climate change.[13] Despite the high levels of waste in western counties, the combination of more people, up to and maybe over 10 billion by the mid 21st Century, and an increasing standard of living equate to an increasing and changing food demand. This applies not only to the basic commodities, such as grains, potatoes, cassava, but especially to white and red meats and dairy products of all types.[14] Logically these demands can be met by either increasing yields from existing land or by expanding the land under cultivation or being grazed. Both options are replete with problems (see Figure 4).

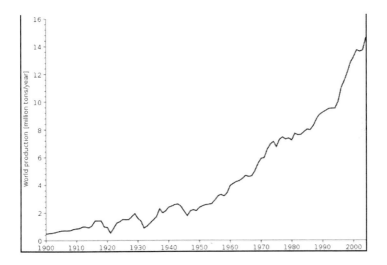

Figure 3a: Trends in world copper production 1900-2007[15]

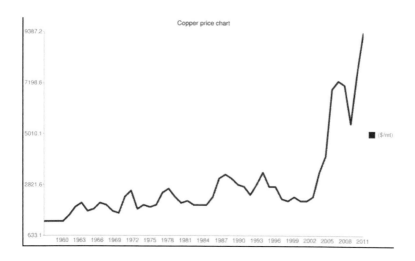

Figure 3b: Copper prices from 1960-2011 ($)

Unused arable land is in short supply and irrigation water even more so. In many regions even existing water supplies are threatened by the over-use of aquifers, rivers or reservoirs and competition from urban demands. Globally about 1.5 billion hectares of land are under cultivation annually, with estimates of the potential area in the range 2 to 4 billion hectares. However, such estimates are fraught as cultivation of inappropriate land can lead to serious difficulties.

Over the last millennium of urban growth and increasing agriculture activity, some 2 billion hectares of farmland have been lost to desertification, salinisation, alkalisation and waterlogging. In the last decade Syria has discouraged the ploughing of the semi-arid 'baadia' because of soil degradation. The 'Garden of Eden' is either desert or salt marsh depending on its exact historic location. Recent urban expansion has increased the pressure. Between 1989 and 1992 China lost 6.5 million hectares to development, while bringing 3.8 million hectares of forest and pasture into cultivation. A large area is lost to the march of urbanization annually, often of the best land. In the USA alone before the financial crunch about 170,000 hectares a year was lost.[16] Worldwide the area probably approaches or may even exceed 1 million hectares.

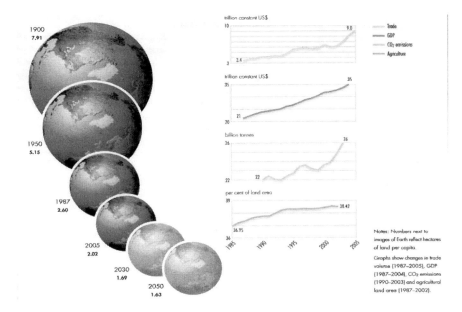

Figure 4: Global Resource Limitations and Use
Source: Global Environment Outlook, *Environment for Development*, United Nations Environment Program 2007.

Worryingly, bringing grassland or forest into arable production is not environmentally cost-free. Ploughing causes oxidization of the soil and the emission of CO_2. As a result an increase in arable land exacerbates the problem of climate change.[17] In addition, important habitats may be lost, watershed flows altered, the capacity of the forest to act as a carbon sink diminished and biodiversity reduced. In short, many ecosystem services are compromised. It is reasonable to conclude that the scope for the sustainable expansion of agricultural land is limited. Indeed, ill-considered expansion has had highly deleterious consequences.

Without doubt there is very substantial scope to improve crop yields and better crop and animal husbandry in many countries. Usually on-farm yields are a poor reflection of those obtained in comparable local, well-managed trials. This applies to both irrigated and rain-fed systems, although historically most of the additional food required to meet the demands of population growth has come from the former. Unfortunately in a number of places, irrigated systems are threatened by diminishing water supplies and urban competition. Moreover, the poor yields have proved resistant to improvement. The problems arise from issues as diverse as land tenure, equitable water rights, farmer education, market access, spiralling debts, cost and availability of agro-chemical inputs, lack of appropriate, well-adapted modern seed, poor quality advice from many National Agricultural Research Systems. Another issue can be the diminished size of farm holdings as land is subdivided between growing family members. Broadly it appears that the easy gains in the most fertile areas have been achieved. Future progress is likely to be won more slowly and more expensively.

Many studies suggest that climate change will reduce water availability in much of the Middle East, Central Asia, Australia and parts of the US, both for rain-fed and irrigated crops.[18] River flow rates are projected to fall in the semi-arid areas, and soil moisture content to decline. Although higher CO_2 levels may stimulate vegetative growth, yields are generally projected to decrease because of greater climatic variability, especially periods of extreme drought, as occurred in Russia in 2010 and Australia in 2008-2011, and catastrophic flooding, as in Pakistan in 2010. Specific phenological issues such as terminal heat stress and poor germination, when rains are late or fail, and decreases in the length of the growing season are a threat. Poorer water availability and greater evapo-transpiration at higher temperatures will combine to limit yields.

Greater intensity and high yields require greater fertility. Less well known is that the application of fertilizer leads to the release of a gas, nitrous oxide (N2O). Unfortunately this is a far more effective greenhouse gas than CO_2 itself (x310 over 100 years). Every tonne of applied nitrogen, whether in the form of manure or inorganic fertilizer, leads to the emissions of about six tonnes of CO_2 equivalent (the total atmospheric forcing of all greenhouse gases is often expressed as CO_2 equivalents - CO_2e).

In addition, commercial fixation of abundant atmospheric nitrogen (N2) gas is itself very energy demanding. The price of the nitrogen fertilizers, so produced, strongly correlates with international oil and gas prices. Since crop yields are near linearly related to the amount of nitrogen available up to several hundred kilograms of nitrogen per hectare, this is not a trivial issue. Paradoxically, the drive for increases in cropping intensity and yield could exacerbate the contribution of the food chain to climate change. Further, the global rate of increase in nitrogen application rivals the increase in atmospheric CO_2 and is ecologically damaging in its own right, leading to eutrophic anoxia in fresh and inshore waters. So intensification is not without cost, and made worse because much of the corn and wheat harvest is fed inefficiently to animals.

The climate change impacts of farm animals and animal products cause much angst in the UK as ruminants such as goats, sheep and cattle, sheep produce a large percentage of global methane (CH_4) emissions. Many of these animals in the US and elsewhere are fed on grain and other concentrates in feed-lots, wastefully diverting resources from direct human use as well as producing methane. On a 100-year basis, methane is about 24 times as effective a greenhouse gas as CO_2. There is no doubt that the world food problem and the global warming impact of the food chain would be reduced dramatically if our diets were to incorporate fewer animal products. We have calculated that, based on current trends in global food demand and population growth, feeding ourselves will **alone** perpetuate climate change and ensure that we breach the +2˚C limit by 2040.[19]

This temperature value is usually considered as a threshold for triggering 'fast-forward' reactions such as the release of tundra methane or added solar radiation absorption from total loss of Arctic summer sea ice. It is important to emphasise that is not simply an issue of about 1.5 billion cattle and other ruminants but as much about the world's population of about 23 billion chickens. The latter have a lower individual greenhouse gas footprint, but collectively are hugely significant in global terms. Moreover, this is without factoring in any tendency to push arable production into unsuitable areas leading to erosion and loss of topsoil and organic matter, or the use of poor quality irrigation water inducing desertification and saline degradation. It is salutary to consider this stark reality even in the unlikely event of mankind being able to completely decarbonize our energy supply by mid century.

Perhaps we are nearing a threshold. Not perhaps an absolute limit but one based on current methodologies, priorities and practices. While staple food prices fell gradually for many decades, in the last years this trend has been reversed. In 2008 a spike in prices triggered food riots in a number of African countries and in the Philippines. Since then, following a small decline, the United Nations Food and Agriculture Organisation's food price index has increased further, reaching 225 in September 2011, compared with its previous peak of 213.5 in June 2008. It's worth recalling that serious unrest caused by food prices in Tunisia and Algeria in early 2011 was a prelude to, perhaps a harbinger of, the Arab Spring.

These examples dramatically illustrate a core message of *The Limits to Growth*. There is no single discrete problem nor is there a unique silver bullet to solve it. Rather we must wrestle with a complex web of interrelated factors - some physical, some social, some political-economic - which together will make the feeding the world's growing population more and more challenging and demand more and more attention and resources.

Paradoxically, if affluence expands then the demands, especially for 'high-end' meat and dairy products, will increase - worsening the climate change threat. Nevertheless the demand from the affluent for agricultural products, including meat, offers access to the market economy and therefore one route out of poverty for the rural poor. Moreover, for many semi-arid, partially nomadic people, pastoral animal-dependent systems are their only option.

In the name of a climatic risk, largely caused by the rich, are we to ban the Masai from herding cattle on the Masai Mara, or the Basutho on the Maloti mountains, or indeed, the graziers of the Welsh hills? Would they and many others listen? How could such policy be imposed? Perhaps we should revert to a near-vegan diet in which case some issues would diminish. Yet the social resistance would be enormous, not just in the US or Australia but in much of Islamic world and Africa. Ethics suggests that we should differentiate between pasturalists who are depending on and using otherwise unused pasture resources, and the cattle and sheep barons heavily dependent on feeding concentrates that compete directly with human use. How could this possibly be achieved? If meat and animal products were to be somehow banned, denial and deceit are inevitable and overshoot a certainty. Moreover, in Galbraithian terms, if the demand for many products, not just red meat but pork, bacon, chicken, turkey, milk, cheese, eggs, yoghurt were to be curtailed, would not many consider that the bargain underpinning affluence had been broken, with incalculable consequences?

We are running on an accelerating treadmill, having to consume more and more time, effort and resources to stop ourselves falling off. Only increasing by 2 per cent annually, our speed doubles in roughly a generation. This growth carries wide environmental consequences as is illustrated by the relationship between GDP and energy use, although above $20,000 per capita wealth the coupling may be reduced (see Figure 5).[20] Demand for goods, even if these are manufactured in China not at home, is a drain on raw materials. Undoubtedly, one factor accelerating the treadmill is population growth, but the other is the Galbraithian bargain which underpins our 'affluent' economy and, much more problematically, the prospects and aspirations of the poor and disadvantaged.[21]

As the demand for resources from a combination of population growth and higher living standards increases, the resilience of food supplies to climatic extremes decreases. At the same time our flexibility to make changes is strangled by the complexity of dealing with not just technical issues but social and politico-economic factors.

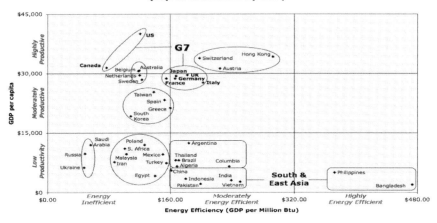

Figure 5. Some relationships of GDP and energy economics
Source: Peter Corless, *Analysis of top 40 largest national economies by plotting GDP per capita versus 'energy efficiency'*, September 2005, published by Wikipedia.

Much as free market zealots argued that the global financial system was largely self-regulating, so critics of *Limits to Growth*, and other similar propositions have declared that, through pricing and scarcity, the market mechanism will stimulate new innovations and circumvent problems. This ignores several factors. Firstly, many incipient problems such as anthropogenic climate change are economic externalities and so excluded from market calculations. This applies not only to atmospheric greenhouse gas emissions but also to the release of nitrogenous and phosphatic compounds into the environment. Secondly, global variation in regulation encourages capital and manufacture to move to the least regulated, usually most pollution-indifferent, low wage location. Thirdly, there is no logical reason to believe that alternatives to scarce resource will always be available. Certainly this applies to food and water. The behaviour of the Chinese government in buying up many of the global copper and other metal resources shows that they are not so complacent. Fourthly, the record shows that the speculative aspect of the free market system ensures that modest changes in supply will be massively magnified by such speculation.

Reaching for sustainability

...truth comes out of error more readily than out of confusion.
Francis Bacon

Sustainability and sustainable development are much abused terms. We need to avoid obviously unsustainable actions such as an exponential increase in ocean fish catches. Such points are well rehearsed in the Meadows' books. But, if our current system is making unsustainable demands on the planet's resources and sinks, even though many are dirt poor and many communities in crisis, what might a more sustainable system look like?

Herman Daly has suggested three criteria for environmental sustainability, distinguishing renewable and non-renewable resource use and pollutant dispersal.[22] For the former he suggests that their rate of use should be no greater than the rate of regeneration or renewal of that source. So, for example, fish catches should be limited to the rate of growth of the fish population, water extraction from an aquifer should not exceed its recharge rate, and farming should not result in a net decline in soil organic matter or net increase in greenhouse gas emissions.

Non-renewable resource use should be no greater than the rate at which a renewable **resource** can be sustainably substituted for it. For instance, oil use could be considered to be sustainable if part of the profit were to be systematically invested in renewable energy sources so that when the non-renewable source is depleted an equivalent renewable source can come on-stream. In the case of a pollutant, the rate of emission should be no higher than the rate at which the pollutant can be recycled, absorbed or rendered harmless, in the way sewage can be degraded by micro-organisms without damaging aquatic ecosystems. One can, perhaps, add to the second Daly criterion that the use of a non-renewable resource should be no greater than the sum of substitution by a renewable resource, as above, **and** the enhanced capacity to recycle and recover the non-renewable resource from waste.

Applying Daly's logic to both nuclear fission power and hydrocarbon fuels is highly uncomfortable. In the case of nuclear power, uranium is a non-renewable resource but given a low supply-risk rating of 4 by the British Geological Survey. Availability at current usage rates appears a modest issue. Should nuclear power become the international electric generating system of choice, regardless of any security considerations, the situation would change dramatically. Supply would rapidly become a problem using current technologies.

However, dealing with the radioactive waste even from the present small number of plants for hundreds or even thousands of years is formidable enough to tax our managerial capacity. Since the 1960s successive UK governments have failed to solve the issue of long-term waste storage.[23] Only after many centuries when the radiation has decayed to a low level does the material become biologically harmless, so fulfilling the Daly's criterion. An international agreement on containment, at a European level at least, is essential. It should be noted here that few who oppose nuclear power, or campaign for 'nuclear free zones' also consider nuclear medicine and the increasing use of radio-nucleids and radio-pharmaceuticals.

In their original 1972 edition of *Limits to Growth*, Meadows and her colleagues were careful to discuss constraints arising both from sources and sinks. Interestingly, reflecting the concerns of the day, they made little of anthropogenic CO_2 emissions (that is, sink impacts) from the use of non-renewable gas, oil and coal resources compared with the future of those reserves themselves. By now it is starkly apparent that both sources and sinks pose problems. Applying Daly's criteria to today's sink data in relation to our hydrocarbon use is truly formidable. Global emissions of the main greenhouse gases would have to return to circa 1870 levels: about 270 ppm for carbon dioxide (from ~390 ppm currently), methane to ~700 ppb (from current ~1800 ppb), and nitrous oxide to 270bpm (from 320 ppb). There is, of course, no prospect of this happening. But the critical issues arise from the continued rapid increases in emissions, and the overshoots and time lags within the system.

Due to the global demand for cheap energy, carbon dioxide emissions illustrate graphically the 'limits' problem in relation to both geophysical and geopolitical reality. There is near-universal, international political agreement that we should strive to avoid a mean global temperature rise of more than 2°C. This roughly equates to atmospheric greenhouse levels of ~450ppm CO_2e – that is, total greenhouse levels expressed as carbon dioxide equivalents. As CO_2e levels are already ~425 ppm, the 450 ppm threshold is certain to be exceeded. The physical problem is that since carbon dioxide is retained in our atmosphere for many decades, it is the **total accumulated carbon dioxide load** that is critical.[24]

If we continue to emit at current rates then the scope for low non-damaging emissions in future decades is diminished. In 2010 global CO_2 emissions reached 35Gt. This represented an increase of record 6 per cent, despite the Kyoto Accord and many protestations of political commitment. International inaction arises from a mixture of short termism and self-interest and is partly compounded by some scientific uncertainty. That is to say, the equating of 450 ppm CO_2e to a ~2°C temperature rise depends on 'global climatic sensitivity'. This refers to how the mean global temperature would rise due a doubling of atmospheric greenhouse gases from pre-industrial levels. The possible figures vary from 4.5 to 1.5°C with a median of ~3°C. This alone gives special interests plenty of scope to sow doubt, even though the global trends are unambiguous. Also we humans have great difficulty distinguishing our local highly variable weather from global climatic trends, or in perceiving time scale.

Historically, 'western' emissions have dominated and our affluence is based on cheap hydrocarbon fuels. Thus it is unsurprising that the rest of the world should expect us to take the initiative and cut our emissions first as they rush to catch up. However, our political leaders are understandably reluctant to tamper with the 'affluence' bargain despite the risks.

Equally, the stance of some in the developing world may be both shortsighted and self-defeating. Countries such as India and China are in the front line for being severely affected by the projected changes. By 2010 global CO_2e emissions per head were about 6 to 7 tonnes.[25] In Wales we emit about 17 tonnes per head. But Chinese emissions have already reached the global mean and they can no longer be counted amongst the innocent. Amongst the innocent are the inhabitants of the low-lying Pacific coral islands who are low carbon emitters but most exposed to sea level rise. The best 'projections' suggest we need to reduce emissions globally to about 2 tonnes per head by 2050, assuming the UN population 'projections'. Few, therefore, can escape their share of responsibility.

Of course, future 'projections' are always difficult to address when 'real politics' is about the here and now. Financial markets deal in profit on a second by second basis. Businesses operate on an annual or multi-year horizon. How can such a system cope with 30 and 40-year 'projections'? How can they deal in scientific probabilities hedged by uncertainty? These problems are surely a recipe for lagged responses and overshoot.

In relation to supply we also face formidable problems. While the concept of 'peak oil' is hotly debated, there is every prospect that oil and gas prices will continue to rise from their current ~$110 per barrel of Brent crude oil, despite the near recession in North America and Europe. Our search for oil takes us deeper and deeper into the oceans and into more problematic territory - the Lula field off Brazil is seven kilometres down. Fracking of tar oils is not only environmentally suspect, but expensive. The commodities director for Barclays, Paul Horsnell, is quoted in New Scientist as forecasting oil at $137 per barrel by 2015 and $185 by 2020.[26] Of course, others differ.

A number of economists have related poor economic growth, in the traditional GDP sense, to high oil prices. It has been suggested that more than 4.5 per cent of GDP is spent on oil in the United States recession ensues. But that figure equates to a price of just $90 per barrel in the United States.[27] So it may be the good news that the price mechanism will force governments, companies and individuals to move rapidly away from oil and gas hydrocarbons. The bad news would be if this meant a rush to coal, a far less greenhouse gas efficient fuel per unit kW produced without carbon capture. This latter unproven technology could, of course, alter the scenario dramatically but would undoubtedly add to costs.

The other reality is that, although there is much talk of developing renewable energy sources and/or nuclear electricity, these are themselves replete with technical, environmental and political problems. The scale of human demand is staggering, of which electricity supply *per se* is only a modest element.

Given our dependence on hydrocarbons, critical questions remain unresolved. Will change occur by the pricing mechanism or by fiat and will it occur fast enough? In physical terms the importance of lags cannot be overstated. Desultory action, which has been made more likely by the outcomes of Copenhagen and Durban climate summits, will probably lead to global CO_2e levels exceeding 550ppm by 2050. This is both dangerous and hugely irresponsible. An unpredictable chain reaction would then be likely to occur, making catastrophic changes possible in a world of 9 to 10 billion people. We would be set on course for a 3 to 4° C mean temperature rise, a massive methane release from the tundra, and a six metre rise in sea level as a result of a major melt of the Greenland ice cap. What then of Bangladesh or the Nile delta or the Fens or indeed low-lying London and New York? Still worse would be any loss of the annual glacial melt which feeds the great Himalayan rivers that sustain billions in India, China and the rest of south and east Asia.

On human frailty

> *Man is practised in disguise; he cheats the most discerning eye.*
> John Gay

It is human to be occasionally dishonest, somewhat hypocritical and capable of self- deceit and self-justification. Psychological experiments show that our honesty is limited and deceases if we feel we enjoy impunity and/or power or, at the very least, an opportunity to escape the consequences of our actions.[28] The least corrupt societies are those with open, well-informed and educated citizens, enjoying freedom of information such as in the liberal social-democratic relatively egalitarian societies of Scandinavia. The broken societies of Iraq, Afghanistan, Burma, and Somalia are worst, while the UK and US lie poised in the middle.

Bribery as a social phenomenon is ingrained in corrupt countries and individuals born into such society are most likely to indulge, even if removed to a new community. But given the close links between power, wealth and corruption, we should be most concerned about the behaviour of powerful, wealthy people. This is because it is the most affluent who might feel they have the most to lose personally from a more sustainable world. They are the ones most able to put out misleading information, buy political influence and invest in inappropriate technologies. Human nature being what it is, no doubt they can also convince themselves that they are acting with integrity and even in the public good.

On the other hand, there is ample psychological and sociological evidence that humans have a keen sense of fairness and justice.[29] In countries where these characteristics are encouraged people appear to enjoy better health and greater fulfillment.

Our current global regime is economically, socially, environmentally, and politically unstable and probably unsustainable. Seeking to maintain and project such a regime into the next 50 to 100 years will almost certainly grossly exceed the planetary limits. Indeed, we may have already done so but our impact is masked by the physical lags. It has been calculated that currently our demands are equivalent to the resources of about one and half Earths. In Wales we may require some three times of our surface area to support us.[30]

Even in this scenario we privileged a few who are deemed, not for very obvious reasons in the case of bankers and many financiers, to be wealth creators. We assume that a version of trickle-down development will improve the living standards of the majority - in the US the so-called 99 per cent. This policy has been singularly ineffective and has resulted in huge discrepancies in income and wealth. Despite attaining national 'affluence', conditions for the poor and many in the middle classes of the USA and UK, the primary cheerleaders for a unfettered free market capitalism, have improved little, if at all, in 40 years.

Meanwhile, Mrs Jones, Llanrug, living on her pension, her equivalent on remittances in the Maloti mountains of Lesotho, or Abdul in his Bangladeshi fishing village have low expectations and low carbon footprints. Yet, although largely blameless compared with the rich or even high-flying scientists, they are more susceptible to rising fuel and food costs and tides. Riches have accrued to a privileged élite who buy power and political influence, and too often peddle half-truths and misinformation about environmental and social issues, avoid paying taxes and even circumvent their legal responsibilities. How can this possibly continue?

It would be facile not to acknowledge the appeal of consumerism and of 'retail therapy', the convenience and appeal of the supermarket or to underestimate our dedication to a particular brand of 'affluence'. Holidays in the sun seem almost a human right. Certainly, they are understandably important to the citizens of the rotting old mill towns or mining villages. All the more so if they are surviving in boring poorly paid jobs in dismal northern European winter weather. As budget airlines will attest, any suggestion that airfares should reflect their full environment cost will be fiercely resisted - the 'bargain' would be jeopardized.

Maybe we are dissatisfied with our materialism and suffering from 'Affluenza'.[31] However, the condition is deeply ingrained and not easily eradicated. We quite enjoy our 'fragile' condition. We may be aware of socially disruptive forces at work in our society, of communities that are marginalised and despairing. But we are swept along on the flood tide of consumerism, taking our holiday while we still can. Can we imagine any other way?

Responses

> The human crisis is always a crisis of understanding;
> what we genuinely understand we can do.
> Raymond Williams

However bleak the situation, it is not axiomatic that the inhabitants of this planet must follow those of Easter Island or Palmyra or indeed many other civilizations to disaster.[32] Some, perhaps many, will retreat into a personal bubble hoping that they and their immediate family can escape or can buy their way out. Others will simply despair and argue that nothing can be achieved. The 'we're all doomed' scenario is corrosive but understandable.

Certainly, allowing the current trends to continue unabated will cause environmental disaster and massive social upheavals. No country or region will be immune. Although northwest Europe is projected to be spared the worst physical threats, our interconnected world makes it inconceivable that we and forthcoming generations will be left to enjoy a quite life unscathed by international social and economic turmoil. There is every probability that, despite the time lags, we are fast approaching a 'limits' crisis - certainly within the lifetimes of our grandchildren, if not earlier.

That being so, the Earth will impose its own logic on humans and human welfare. Although masters of self-deception, we cannot 'cheat' or deceive the bio and geo-chemical cycles that control life on our planet. No doubt many will emerge chastened to reignite human culture. In my judgment the overriding issue is not 'limits' per se, but whether we can navigate a transition to a sustainable global future in a humane and relatively orderly way. The alternative is that the transition will occur brutally and chaotically, as suggested by James Lovelock in his *The Vanishing Face of Gaia: The Final Warning* (2009).

We will have to work very hard to achieve a softish landing. If we stopped to consider it, humankind has an overwhelming vested interest in reducing its environmental impacts. However, as so often with the 'common good', it is questionable whether we are capable of rising above our narrow personal, sectoral and national interests. Are there ways we can be motivated to do so? Quoting Gramsci - we must harness 'the optimism of the will' despite 'the pessimism of the intellect'. Human environmental impact can be represented (30) as:

$$Impact = Population \times Affluence \times Technology.[33]$$

Each factor is important and deserves serious analysis.

Population

First, consider population and the implications for energy and greenhouse gas emissions as a specific exemplar. It is obvious, but in my experience never admitted by politicians, that the larger the human population then the lower are the individual emissions compatible with limiting global climate change to about +2°C (or indeed any other target). It will also be harder to achieve such a target. The same applies, equally obviously, to demand for resources such as food and water (see also Figures. 2 and 4).

As noted earlier, total but rapidly rising emissions of about 45 Gt CO_2e in 2010 equate to about 6-7 tonnes per head. But by 2050 total global emissions need to be reduced to about 15 to 18 tonnes. If, as anticipated, the population has reached 9 to 10 billion, this equates to 1.5 to 2 tonnes each. Currently in Wales we are individually responsible for about 17 CO_2e tonnes, so we must look to about a 90 per cent cut (assuming a constant population of 3 million). From this perspective, everyone has a huge interest in curbing population growth, locally, nationally, and globally. If at all possible, the global population should not exceed 8 to 9 billion, despite the teachings of the Pope, some Islamic leaders and true believers in the miraculous powers of unfettered capitalism.

Experience suggests that population control is best achieved by female education, empowerment and enfranchisement. Indeed, that is a win-win situation for all but the most reactionary. However, a growing population creates additional demands for electricity, housing and other resources and facilities and can lubricate GDP growth. Populous cities are often generators of economic growth, while rural depopulation brings a raft of problems. But this thrust can only diminish our chances of meeting even the official target of an 80 per cent greenhouse gas cut by 2050. It is nevertheless quite remarkable that a developed country such as the UK seems incapable of producing its own skilled professionals and senior industrialists. Instead, it relies on importing medical and technical expertise, nurses and carers, plumbers and information technologists, and even bankers and traders from other often much poorer counties.

Ceasing population growth has profound economic and social implications for individual nations and also globally, especially when linked to a longer life expectancy. The proportion of those of working age will decline and of the aged increase. Those in their fifties and sixties will be expected to work for significantly longer, possible blocking employment and advancement for the young and middle aged. The problem of pensions will be acute, especially if stock market values stall, as is likely if the Galbraithian bargain unravels. But perhaps the bleakest prospects arise from the failure of healthy active old age to keep pace with absolute longevity. Thus the number and the time span of those requiring support and care will increase more rapidly than the actual number of over seventies. In the UK the historic answer has been to import labour, especially young labour, to build, nurse and care. This is not readily compatible with sustainable development as it denudes other societies of the skills they need. On the other hand, it is an area where much employment could be generated and human welfare enhanced at low environmental cost if ways can be found to pay those involved a reasonable wage.

Technology

To achieve a more sustainable and stable regime, technological enterprise and initiatives are essential. Some hanker after a 'simple' solution, a reversion to small self-sufficient communities. This may have worked (partially) for a global population of a less than a billion prior to 1800 but for one an order of magnitude greater in 2050, it would be highly problematical. Few would wish to return to a period in history when the great majority lived in squalor. At that time our ambition was to escape from the horror of a subsistence hand to mouth existence.

Such scenarios may arise from major catastrophes, but not from choice. It is not even clear that localism in food chains or, were it feasible, a dependence on entirely local production will ensure the lowest carbon footprint. Should Wales or regions therein, seek to achieve self-sufficiency in grain, for example, the consequential ploughing of grassland would increase CO_2e emissions significantly for decades. Nevertheless there is indeed room for more local exchanges, better food chains and a 'reinvention' of seasonal food. At all times the priority must be a low greenhouse gas footprint and a sustainable economy, not romance.

We must privilege technological changes, inventions and companies that reduce human environmental impacts. Paradoxically, although modern free market capitalism is at the core of both our transient affluence and our environmental problems, we must seek to harness its dynamism to generate the tools to extract humanity from the hole into which it has dug itself. Given our capacity for self-deception and cheating this will not be easy and rigorous criteria must be applied and audited.

However, an appreciation of the logic of exponential growth is of value. In becoming the workshop of the world the Chinese economy has been growing at just below 10 per cent a year - that is, doubling in eight to nine years. Even if significant resource decoupling is achieved, demand for hydrocarbon energy or copper or other raw material can be expected to double in 12 to 18 years. Hence, their policy of buying as many raw material sources in Africa and South America as possible. Clearly China does not take the view that resource constraints are unimportant or adopt a pure free market perspective that human technological invention will always find alternatives or substitutes.

Energy is central. Meadows and colleagues recognised the importance of harnessing technology to produce renewable low greenhouse gas emitting energy. They acknowledged the need to move towards a new hydrogen and electricity economy, to reduce energy use and increase energy use efficiency. Let us recall in this sector we are talking about reducing mean **per capita** global emissions from all sectors of energy generation and use, including aircraft, ships, vehicles, space heating, industrial processes such as cement manufacture, and the whole of the food chain, from between 6-7 tonnes in 2010, to 1.5 to 2 tonnes by 2050. A new global Marshall plan will be required. Is it too naive to point out that we invest each year globally some $1.5 trillion dollars in armaments and the military (the USA alone nearly $700 billion) and that foreign exchange transactions (largely speculation) amount to $955 trillion? The world would be much safer and fairer if a sizable fraction were invested in technologies to increase environment sustainability as defined by Daly. Might such a shift not create much more valuable and rewarding work than currently obtains? Can we create an enviro-industrial complex as powerful as the military-industrial complex?

The overriding question is simply this: do we take 'limits' seriously? These should include all the Earth's renewable and non-renewable resources and the strength and availability of sinks and dispersal times. If we were to do so, then I would readily join the optimists and would be confident that science, technology and human ingenuity would achieve an orderly transition. But to do so requires a new paradigm, a complete rethink and overhaul of our political and financial systems, and unprecedented global cooperation. The new system would need to put bio and geo-chemical 'limits' as its key criterion against which all activities are assessed, not as an incidental add-on. Therein lies the rub. Can such a change be contemplated?

Gross Domestic Product (GPD) has little to commend it as a measure of human welfare or even personal economic success, a view that its originator recognized.[34] GDP is equal to the sum of private consumption, gross investment, government spending, and exports minus imports) within a particular area. Its inadequacies are apparent. After all, if one were to move 30 miles further from work to a large drafty house with a huge heating bill then one would be increasing one's contribution to GDP while diminishing one's own living standard. Going to prison might make a further contribution, especially if it meant either the state or private enterprise building a new one. If forest clearance in an upper watershed leads to downstream flooding, expensive insurance claims and an investment in major flood control schemes, they would all contribute commensurately to GDP.

Nevertheless, despite its lack of discrimination, there appears to be a broad correlation between GDP and the ability of an economy to create jobs, generate tax income and sustain the business of government. However, it is no guide to sustainability. Aside from its indifference to human welfare, the exclusion of environmental externalities - be that air quality in Liverpool, loss of biodiversity, flood risk or climate change - GDP will only change when the purchase price of an item is altered or an investment made.

It is almost designed to encourage overshoot.

Various efforts have been made to modify GDP to better reflect the real world such as the Index of Sustainable Economic Welfare (ISEW), the Genuine Progress Indicator (GPI) and the UN System of Integrated Environmental and Economic Account.[35] For example, in ISEW, personal consumption (as measured in GDP above) is modified by the addition of public non-defensive expenditures but reduced by private defensive expenditure, for example a need for private policing or to fit CCTV or burglar alarms. Capital formation is added as are services for domestic labour (ignored in GDP), while estimates of environmental degradation and the depreciation of 'natural capital' are subtracted. The treatment of 'natural capital' such as oil reserves, soil or biodiversity as income is one of the main criticisms highlighted by Schumacher in his famous book, *Small is Beautiful.*[36]

It is apparent from these paragraphs that, despite its obvious deficiencies, any move away from GDP poses a major political and intellectual challenge. Politicians, especially in democracies where shelf lives are short, are as hooked on GDP as our society is on cheap energy. Many of the additional measurements and data required are difficult to acquire and are potentially contentious. Would not different factions value wind-turbines very differently even if there was an agreed price for their electricity and CO_2 emission reductions? Politically, it is easy to imagine rival parties parading a raft of often-spurious arguments while the public, with its ingrained scepticism, would wonder if this was not a massive con. Perhaps our obsession with placing a monetary value on everything is a symptom of our malaise? Is pandering to it part of the problem? Nevertheless it can be asserted with confidence that sustainable development cannot be made a 'central organizing principle' if GDP is retained as the measure of economic development and its associated growth remains a vital policy objective.

Fairness is the critical issue. Affluence has entailed seeking to emulate an élite - keeping up with the neighbours, acquiring better cars, and more and longer holidays. In this pursuit our society becomes more unequal. Income disparities and working hours for those in work have soared. We have acquiesced in the expectation that it is the price to be paid for maintaining or even increasing affluence, and turning Galbraith's treadmill. The 'wealth-maker' rewards could hypothetically be justified, even welcomed, if their efforts allowed the rest to enjoy a rising standard of living: a version of the much criticized theory of international development known as 'trickle-down' development. However, these pretensions have been dissipated and the balloons pricked.

Regrettably it appears that the less affluent will be paying a disproportionate amount of the bill to pay off debt and bail out the financial services sector. I am not aware of any senior executive in the financial services sector who has been required to face the legal consequences of their greed and deceit. In the mean time, we must also expect rising energy and food costs to further disadvantage the disadvantaged. Galbraith also suggests that a highly unequal society finds it hard to maintain the bargain and keep the consumer wheel turning. He observed that the middle and lower income groups could be relied upon to spend their income on goods and services and not to hoard unproductively, whereas the elite super rich are under no such pressure.[37] Perhaps the 'limits' are creeping up on us in unanticipated ways.

Sustainability and equity have to be close partners, with all this implies for policy in Wales, within the UK, within Europe and globally. For example, it requires that greenhouse gas emissions must be addressed per head. Should people or nation be inclined after such a point to increase their population, would it not be equitable to cap their total emissions? If an individual has compelling reasons for a larger share, s/he will have to buy it from the spare capacity of others. Similarly fair taxes would have to be paid by all and tax havens abolished. Currently it appears that the poor need to be galvanized to work hard by their lowly status and by freezing their wages, while the rich need tax breaks to encourage them to work harder.

Humanity

Hope is not the conviction that something will turn up, but the certainty that something makes sense regardless of how it turns out.
Vaclav Havel

At the heart of the problem lie the relationships between our political-economic regime, our human natures, our moral codes and our ethical and religious value systems, and the natural world. In recent decades greed has been declared good. The super-rich, be they bankers, sport stars or celebrities are lauded and seen as role models. In parts of the USA even Jesus is deemed to make believers rich and successful. He appears to partake of the American dream, consort with American exceptionalism and to be a guarantor of security. More prosaically in the UK, WAGs (wives and girlfriends) are synonymous with conspicuous consumption, bankers, rock stars and footballers with excess. All but the bankers are regarded as desirable role models.

In following their leads we have plunged into debt but gained little satisfaction. How very different from the values of Welsh society a few decades ago and the values espoused by virtually all humanities, great thinkers and sages including of course Jesus. Setting aside Galbraith's insights and recommendations, our partly mythical affluence has been built on debt, both as individuals and as a country (now totaling nearly 500 per cent of UK GDP) and on exploiting natural capital. Individual welfare is being rapidly and painfully eroded. Despite its heavy environmental and social cost, our recent 'affluence' was partly a mirage. The 'emperor' had few clothes. The huge social cost and the betrayal of post war aspirations by casino capitalism has inspired Stephane Hessel to 'Outrage' and the 'occupy Wall Street' movement.[38]

Much has been written about the 'tragedy of the commons', that is the relative ease with which common group assets are mismanaged and denuded.[39] This appears a persuasive analogy for the problem of atmospheric greenhouse gas pollution and consequential climate change, or maybe even the stripping out of global capital assets for the benefit of a few. But there are differences:

- It is not a commonly owed resource but an un-owned resource upon which, nevertheless, we all depend.
- The effects of the pollution will not be consistent throughout the Earth nor experienced equally by people.
- The atmosphere and climate, both local and global, as un-owned resources, encourage free loaders and individual countries and sectors to plead their special cases.

Worse we face intergenerational inequity with our generation of the 'affluent' acting as free loaders at the expense of their children. In the cases of common land and un-owned global resources, the danger of others benefiting whilst we 'do the right thing' is a real dilemma – potentially, making a mockery of any 'sacrifice'.

In moving forward we need to honestly inform citizens about our human predicament, as this is perhaps the only way to ensue a measure of compliance. It will not be easy. We have singularly failed to hold the city financiers and traders to account. Feted by Labour, new and old, Tories of all complexions and Lib Dems alike, the City élite has every reason to feel smug and untouchable. Consequently people are deeply sceptical and cynical. Although the old order must be changed, it is difficult to conceive of a scenario where a London government will act decisively. Paradoxically, our economic malaise gives bankers, financiers and industrialists more power. Individually and collectively we are desperate for our town or region or children to benefit from some windfall investment or new jobs. Similarly government is desperate to avoid major companies relocating and, at the very least, to maintain its tax take.

Short of a totalitarian response, perhaps our only hope lies in the democracy and openness of the web. The Animal Farm model of governance tempts all-powerful leaders, whether they start as communist, fascist, Welsh nationalist, Valley's Labour or old Etonian. Power not only corrupts but blinds. The crisis of 'limits' can only increase the chances of an authoritarian leadership. What price democracy in Greece or Italy when staring at the abyss of economic collapse? What price the rights of workers if the Government response to the crisis is to make it easier for companies to sack their staff?

Faced with these choices, our three Westminster parties and US Republicans and Democrats have all chosen to save the banks and bankers, fearing even worse disaster. Only 'people power' can hold government, power brokers and polluters to account. Only the people can achieve the paradigm shift required to attain even a measure of sustainability. For this they must be convinced that it is in their and their families' best interests and that comparative justice will be done. Can we avoid lurching into a neo-fascist state? Can we achieve an orderly transition or will it be disorderly and brutal, as predicted by James Lovelock amongst others? Can we harness human energy and creativity, so apparent in self-interested capitalism, not to exploit the planet's resources but to maximise long-term human welfare and satisfaction? In asking these questions we must recognize an acute dilemma, that the currently rich, powerful and influential will be the biggest losers in the short run.

For Wales see Cymru

> "... to be truly radical is to make hope possible rather than
>   despair convincing."
> Raymond Williams

The 1998 and 2006 Government of Wales Acts stipulated the pursuit or promotion of 'sustainable development'. Elected in May 2011 the current Welsh Government not only intends to make sustainable development 'its central organizing principle' but to embed it in primary legislation. This is therefore a crucial opportunity to establish effective principles to ensue long-term progress. In addition to providing intergenerational equity, sustainable development is often interpreted as a triple bottom line of a 'viable successful economy' supporting 'vibrant communities' in ways, which are 'environmentally sustainable'. The objective is to create a culturally and economically successful country to be inherited by our children and children's children. This is, of course, greatly to be welcomed but the implications have not yet been explored nor, I would suggest, widely understood. This essay is intended as a contribution to this dialogue but we are many years from an economy which is truly sustainable in economic, social or environment terms.

Even without addressing many vital community and cultural issues, the discussion to date has demonstrated the size and complexity of the challenge. A serious attempt to grapple with the issues is found in Tim Jackson's book *Prosperity Without Growth* which is based on the conclusions of the UK Sustainable Development Commission disbanded in 2011.[40] However, if we are approaching – and possibly have reached - global 'limits' internationally, these will tend to define spending priorities. Inevitably such a crisis will re-orientate activity towards mitigating the social and economic damage inflicted by the breached 'limits', and towards securing adequate work, energy, food and related goods and services and social support. It appears that the international debt crisis is already carrying us down such path. However, regardless of current preoccupations, we have only a few decades to find sustainable paths and solve the paramount problem of reducing our greenhouse gas emissions drastically. How, therefore, can a country relatively low in the affluence league in European terms, with limited fiscal and policy levers, move forward? Are there practical ways of approaching a sustainable form of development, and achieving a realistically based prosperity for Wales? Can we take a lead, much as we did during the industrial revolution of the 19th Century?

I suggest we need to distinguish short-term, urgent actions that can be pursued locally and immediately from a longer-term comprehensive strategy. Also, although some initiatives can be pursued within the National Assembly's current powers, others will depend on acquiring additional powers to allow Wales to increase its sustainability. Critically, and despite people's distrust of authority and jaundiced view of politicians, their trust must be won. In many contexts the 'expert' does not always know best; certainly this is the common feeling. Initiatives should be informed by but not led by so-called 'experts' or 'consultants'. In Wales, where there isn't a strong tradition of 'institutions', we need to find ways of motivating citizens to take action for themselves, trusting to their common sense, not nannying.

Wales has a few modest comparative advantages. Fortunately we are not in hock to the financial services sector and, hopefully, are less anti-European than our English neighbours. Hopefully, we can recognise that many facets of sustainable development can best be achieved within an active cooperative European framework and that we have much to learn from initiatives outside the UK. Only on such a broad canvas may we be able to create a sufficiently powerful economic zone of common laws, regulations and ambitions to promote fairness, protect individual rights and the environment and provide a mechanism to counterbalance the destructive powers of big business and high finance.

Certainly, the successful pursuit of enhanced sustainability demands action at all levels - international, EU, UK, Welsh and local. Some, such as regulation of emissions from air and sea travel, carbon trading and potentially carbon taxes can only be contemplated meaningfully at the EU level. Other issues around the management and reliability of electrical supply through the National Grid have a vital UK and cross channel component. Similarly, action at an UK or British and Irish level is required in matters such as inter-conurbation travel and regulating the City. Although from a Welsh perspective we have little direct influence, we must ensure that our voice is heard.

Fortunately, Wales still retains a sense of communal cohesion and is sufficiently small to sustain an internal dialogue and debate about these issues and achieve a measured response, which could be even more problematical in large heterogeneous country. In his *Small is Beautiful* Schumacher did not argue exclusively for 'smallness'. Rather, he observed that our allegiance to the gargantuan can be misplaced. He argued that the human scale was the most appropriate. Interestingly, Cymry means 'fellow members of a group in which negotiated outcomes are possible'. Welsh on the other hand is the English word for 'others'. We need to see ourselves as 'cymrodyr', 'y Cymry', and not defined by otherness. We have potentially a highly educated and motivated population with deep cultural and historic roots. An unappreciated facet of Welsh life is our closeness to the rural world. Even in Cardiff people are within easy reach of the countryside. Nowhere is but a few miles from a rural or coastal area or a National Park. If, as I would conclude, the emerging sustainable economy will seek inspiration and individuals find solace and enjoyment from clear ties with the natural world, then we in Wales are extremely fortunate.

We have good natural resources in terms of renewable energy, water, timber and food, especially pasture-derived animal products, as well as a long history of technological innovation and scientific research. However, to date moves to utilize these assets effectively have been uncertain and hampered by the division of responsibility between the Welsh Government and Westminster.

Historically, Wales has lacked many essential economic and political levers, although our comparative impotence makes us representative of many other nations and regions. This was partially rectified by the successful referendum on legislative powers for the Assembly in March 2011. Additional powers will required in relation to our natural resources. At the same time, the new low impact technologies that will emerge cannot be contained in a region or single nation. Research findings are by their nature international but if well focused can provide local or national advantage. In the remainder of this essay I will concentrate on national and local actions, while recognising that supra-national action may lag, as exemplified both by the comparative failure of climate change negotiations at Copenhagen and Durban.

Given the depth of the global challenge and our small geographic, economic and political space, Wales needs to address not only **mitigation** – that is, how to play our part in limiting the emission of pollutants and the irresponsible use of resources - but also **adaptation** and **resilience**. The former addresses ways to lighten the impact of impending crises such as peak oil on our society, and the latter ways we can increase our national capacity to withstand sudden, unexpected storms.

Daly defines an environmentally sustainable system as one with a 'steady state economy'. This is one which retains a constant stock of physical capital, which does not erode its own natural resources or those of elsewhere by its imports, in a world that enjoys a rate of material through-put within its regenerative capacities and adsorptive capabilities. While one cannot fault this logic, we are light years from achieving it and to move precipitously to this condition would be invite danger and could be counter-productive. The Daly criteria have the advantage of being quantifiable but do not extend readily to economic, social and cultural issues.

As a working definition in a Welsh context, sustainable development can be considered a political-economic system which promotes human prosperity through a range of work opportunities and the provision of quality services in and through the private and public sectors, while:

• Progressively adhering to the Daly principles of environmental sustainability.
• Enhancing cultural and social activities, including specifically through the medium of the Welsh language.
• Conserving biological diversity and natural beauty.
• Stimulating vigorous communities of self-confident compassionate individuals.

If this can be accepted, then we need a broadly agreed strategy to progress to such sustainability over 20 years. This, I suggest, implies a sequence away from Anglo-American casino-capitalism, first to a Nordic-style social democratic, mixed economy. This should entail an enhanced and continuing decoupling of a redefined growth model away from energy use and production, from the emission of greenhouse gases and from the production of wasteful rubbish and other pollutants. Over several decades this would lead to a fully decoupled 'steady state' economy by 2030 to 2040. It must be emphasized that decoupling *per se* is not straightforward and can be dangerously misconstrued.

For example, technological innovations can increase output at lower financial and environmental cost. But any gains could be overwhelmed if demand consequently increases substantially. On a personal level, we might invest to improve the energy efficiency of our homes, so saving on heating costs. However, if these savings were then spent on extra flights to Spain or longer car journeys, all the good work would be undone. Consequently public understanding and consent, although currently largely absent, is essential.

There can be little disagreement that energy supply and use and the attendant mitigation of greenhouse gas emissions lie at the heart of the sustainability issue. Energy costs are embedded throughout all aspects of the economy. Virtually everything revolves around energy: from housing to transport to industrial production and the food chain. As early as the 1960s intensive agriculture was recognised to be essentially a method of converting oil into food.[41]

The public may be more open to arguments about **adapting** to the increasing cost and likely insecurity of electricity and fuel supply than the more esoteric prospect of **mitigating** our overshooting the capacity of the atmospheric carbon sink. Few will volunteer to do away with the 'convenience' of their own freewill, so interventions will need to be tailored to this fact. Self-interest can be aligned with 'sustainability' and government must apply a judicious use of both sticks and carrots to achieve this.

A further note of caution is needed. The scenarios discussed earlier seem to imply that the service economy should offer low greenhouse gas economic returns but even this can be misleading. Carbon foot-printing of Gwynedd found that, given its reliance on motor vehicles tourism made a very large contribution.[42] Sadly the Snowdonia Green Key project, which might have provided part of the solution, has floundered due to lack of imagination, communication skills and political will. The lesson is not that tourism should be discouraged but that every effort should be made in all sectors to create and promote attractive and credible options with low greenhouse gas footprints.

My objective is to broaden a practical and evidence-based debate that leads to setting some strategic initiatives for Wales, given our serious economic, social and environmental deficiencies. The concepts below are predicated on expanding the local and regional components of the economy, increasing the social and cooperative elements to provide greater resilience, and enhancing personal environmental responsibility. In pursing the objective of 'sustainable development' as our 'central organising principle' we should acknowledge that the private, public and social enterprise spheres will each have unique and complementary roles. Each will have to contribute to job creation but it is highly unlikely that we can deliver a pure, free enterprise, low tax, and low spend system. Nevertheless all must meet criteria for sound economic management. Isolationism is not an option. Continued trade will be vital. Enterprise must be encouraged but with a re-balancing to favour local multipliers. In the medium term the Welsh Government must:

1. Commit the country and government to adopt the principles of 'one planet' living which would embed the following ten features:

   - Zero Carbon
   - Zero Waste
   - Sustainable transport
   - Sustainable materials
   - Local and sustainable food
   - Sustainable water
   - Land use, wildlife and ecosystems
   - Language, culture and heritage
   - Equity and inclusion
   - Health and happiness

2. Commit to using a version of the Index of Sustainable Welfare, which measures sustainable growth and properly 'subtracts' negative actions that destroy natural, social and cultural capital. The move from casino capitalism to true sustainability cannot be navigated without better analytical tools, both to develop new innovative policies and technologies, and to allocate scarce resources. First and foremost, this requires the adoption of more discriminatory economic tools and a better 'real growth' measurement than GDP to guide investment and policy. Valuable work has been already been carried out on a Sustainable Economic Welfare index for Wales and measuring 'progress' at an European level.[43] These must be built on.

3. Acquire real power over energy, planning and transport. This would entail a statutory power over Ofgen in Wales and the regulation of energy distribution to facilitate public involvement in dispersed renewable energy production and energy saving. We will also need to develop planning tools to ensure better energy conservation, and provide much firmer controls of car-based, out-of-town developments. We should give serious consideration to a 60mph speed limit on dual carriageways. In the medium term we should establish a network of electrical and later hydrogen charging stations for vehicles. To make good use of the Welsh Government's enhanced powers a larger elected membership is essential for rigorous policy analysis and scrutiny. In addition high quality, dedicated public servants are necessary. The Government should encourage civil servants to be more proactive and innovative. The current divided-loyalty between Cardiff and Whitehall must be resolved. Finally the Welsh Government must accept the challenge of responsibility for its own research budget.

4. Establish a 'regional' Bank on the lines of those in North Dakota or the German Lander to retain local savings and support sustainable local business, industry and commerce. This would recognise the twin issues of improving the local economy in the face of the centripetal and income-lowering forces of globalisation and mobile City investment, and of stimulating low environmental impact growth and employment. We should provide legal and commercial advice to companies on structures that could protect them from unwelcome external takeovers. The Glas Cymru mutual model that operates Welsh Water in one example. It is interesting, both the Bank of England and the World Bank have recently recognised that the impacts of the free flow of capital, unfettered company relocation and aggressive take-overs are not necessarily positive.

5. Reinvigorate the Welsh local economy by using the purchasing power of the Welsh Government, local authorities, and related bodies such universities, schools, colleges and hospitals to support local business and increase local multipliers. We should resolve once and for all the conflict between benefiting the local economy and a slavishly over-stringent interpretation of European procurement law.[44]

6. Promote public engagement, fairness, language, culture and justice. In general and in its current form, sustainable development has a bad press. Many, perhaps the great majority, regard it as a threat to their lives and aspirations, and as an excuse for more interference by government and highhanded individuals. While the current crisis in 'conventional capitalism' may have soured their view of that system, few can conceive of any other. Hence the desperate demands for

GDP growth. In current 'conventional thinking' it seems inconceivable that an environmentally responsible, truly sustainable economy could be fulfilling and offer exciting prospects to the ambitious and hard working. Nevertheless, the exploitative unjust core of the current unsustainable system is so obvious that we have David Cameron and Ed Miliband competing on how to curb its excesses.

Of course, social justice is not a uniquely Welsh concept. However, we have a proud legacy in the ideas of Robert Owen, Lloyd George and Aneurin Bevan as well as countless trade union and religious leaders, including St David's reputed commitment to doing small communal actions 'gwnewch y pethau bychain'. As Michael Sandell argues, justice does not eliminate value judgments but requires them.[45] Fairness and social justice between generations, nations and people, with a strong emphasis on social and individual responsibility, lie at the heart of sustainable development.

In some ways it is all very Welsh! Instead of competing for new toys and gadgets, we should express our human competitiveness through sports, culture, the arts and sciences. This is entirely compatible with the Welsh eisteddfod tradition. As well as being an important component of our heritage, the Welsh language should be a stimulus to individual and social enterprises and local entrepreneurs. In many ways, its future is a measure of our sustainability. The negative forces undermining the language are frequently those that reduce the sustainability of development. Only with vibrant, self confident communities can a minority language itself flourish. We should embrace bilingualism, not just for those who currently speak Welsh, but as part of all our heritages.

Epilogue

> ...there is wealth only in people and in their land and seas. Uses of wealth which abandon people are so profoundly contradictory that they become a social disaster, on a par with the physical disasters, which follow from reckless exploitation of land and seas.
> Raymond Williams

This essay argues that our core problem arises from the highly successful, selectively trans-formative, economic system that has evolved initially in the West over the last few hundred years. It has created unprecedented affluence for a proportion of humanity, while centralising power and money in élites, encouraging irrational exuberance, and ensuring overshoot. The system commits society, both globally and regionally, to infinite exponential growth. Measured by GPD, this growth is insensitive to the erosion of natural, social and cultural capita and indifferent to the source of capital, be it debt finance, money printed by government or financial perfidy.

The system contains the seeds of its own destruction. It is seductive but unsustainable. Nowhere is this more apparent than in the energy-climate change crisis. The forces sucking the life out of our mining and quarrying communities, eroding the Welsh language and hurtling us globally toward damaging climate change are inextricably intertwined. In time the planetary bio-geo-physical realities will reassert themselves, undoubtedly with unanticipated consequences. Major technological feats, such a new low carbon energy sources may be developed but can only buy time for a more profound reappraisal and allow space for adjustment. Just as the robust certainties of Newtonian physics have been overtaken by the subtle strangeness of Einsteinian quantum physics, and pre-Darwin-Wallace-Mendel natural history transformed into modern evolutionary and molecular biology, a new social-economic paradigm must be sought.

Given the magnitude of the challenge and pressure of current economic and social problems, even in this country, still more in the developing world, the understandable and inevitable reaction of politicians is to plump for conventional growth - to seek economic space for readjustment. Sustainability is seen as a distant desirable objective - 'Oh God make me sustainable but not just yet'! This is a sure receipt for overshoot. Much more work is required to map out a 20-year pathway to a new paradigm. First, however, we must face the issues honestly. This is a process that cannot start too soon.

The new paradigm will not be anti-business or anti-science. Innumerable opportunities will occur for enterprise and new businesses, which lower human environmental impact and increase real individual prosperity and facilitate social interactions. Dispersed renewable energy generation could be the key as it would provide local additional income sources and personalise the attainment of sustainability, including energy efficiency.

At the same time it will underscore the scale of the problem. We will be very hard pressed to be energy self-sufficient and, will be unlikely to solve the issue of energy storage. We need action at various levels, both technically and politically. A sustainable future is not anti-technology, nor low on ingenuity. Indeed it is quite the opposite. But the economic incentives and disincentives must be consistent with lessening our global and local impacts. We need to work with the grain of bio-geo-physical constraints and not in defiance of them. Some of the essential levers to effect such a change will lie in Wales, others do not and will not.

Many brilliant minds are engaged in maintaining the Galbraithian bargain and in advertising and promoting our 'wants'. It is not inconceivable that these talents and our growing understanding of human psychology can be used to encourage a far less destructive system. It is also entirely probable that such systems will create a greater degree of real well-being and contentment. This essay started by contrasting the apparent optimism of the advocates of unfettered 'growth' with the pessimism of the doom-mongers. I suggest this is simplistic and misleading. Rather we should be dismayed by attempts to prop up a destructive system. Despite the huge challenges we should enthuse about the prospects for real human prosperity and fulfilment from making the change to the new paradigm of sustainable development.

Notes

1   This essay is dedicated to my four grandsons, Euros, Aled, Eirig and Owain hoping that, in 50 years time, they will be understanding of the follies of older generations and have lived through non-catastrophic change. I am grateful to Dr Havard Prosser, Professor Ross Mackay, Dr James Intriligator, Dr Dafydd Trystan, and especially Dr Einir Young for their comments and suggestions for this essay. The faults are, of course, mine alone.

2   See Rees, Martin, *Our Final Century: Will the human race survive the 21st century?* Heinemann, 2003; Lovelock, James, *The Vanishing Face of Gaia: The Final Warning*, Penguin, 2009; and Flannery, Tim, Now or Never: Why we need to act now for a sustainable future, Harper, 2009.

3   Galbraith, John Kenneth, *The Affluent Society*, Pelican, 1958.

4   Meadows, Donella. H. et al., *The Limits to Growth*. Earth Island, 1972.

5   Meadows, D.H. et al., *Beyond the Limits*, Chelsea Green, 1992; and Meadows, D.H. et al., *Limits to Growth: 30 year update*, Earthscan, 2005.

6   http://www.storyofstuff.org/movies-all/story-of-stuff/

7   Hawranek, Dieter et al., *Out of Control: The destructive power of financial markets*, Der Spiegel-on-line, 22 August 2011.

8   Chakraborthy, A., writing in *The Guardian*, quoting the Centre for Research on Socio-Cultural Change, University of Manchester, 13 December 2011.

9   Meadows, Donella. H. et al., *The Limits to Growth*. Earth Island, 1972

10   Montreal Protocol on Substances that Deplete the Ozone Layer, UNEP, Kenya, 2000.

11   Hogan, C.M., *Overfishing*, Encyclopedia of Earth. NCSE, Washington D.C., 2010.

12   British Geological Survey, *Risk List 2011*.

13   See papers on the International Food Policy Institute web site, especially those of Mark Rosegrant, 2010-11. See also the websites of the Climate, agriculture and food security organisation and the Consultative Group on International Agricultural Research, for instance. http://www.cgiar.org/pdf/CCAFS_Strategy_

december2009.pdf

14   See the United Nations' Food and Agriculture Organisation's online datasets, available at http://faostat. fao.org/site/380/default.aspx 2010.

15   http://en.wikipedia.org/wiki/File:Copper_-_world_production_trend.svg

16   Meadows, D.H. et al., *Limits to Growth: 30 year update*, Earthscan, 2005.

17   R.K. Pachauri, A. Reisinger, (Eds.), Contribution of Working Groups I, II and III to the Fourth Assessment Report of the Intergovernmental Panel on Climate Change, 2007. Also IPCC (1996) Revised 1996 IPCC Guidelines for National Greenhouse Gas Inventories, Intergovernmental Panel on Climate Change, www. ipcc.ch, 1996; and Intergovernmental Panel on Climate Change Emissions Databases, 2010: available at http://www.ipcc-nggip.iges.or.jp/EFDB/main.php

18   *Ibid.*

19   Wyn Jones, R. Gareth et al. (2012) *Climatic mitigation, adaptation and dryland food production*, Proceedings of the International Dryland Development Commission 2010 Conference, Cairo, 2012; see also Taylor, Rachel. C. et al., *Before 2050 human food chain will drive climate change*.

20   Organisation for Economic Co-operation and Development, *Towards Green Growth: monitoring progress*, 2011.

21   *Per capita* UK energy use is growing at about 1 per cent a year. Given the population continues to rise, total use has grown faster - despite outsourcing emissions to China and elsewhere by our importing of manufactures and food containing 'embedded' greenhouse gases.

22   Daly, H., 'Institutions for a Steady State Economy', in *Steady State Economics*. Island Press, 1991.

23   The Dutch have been more successful with their short-term (100-year) repository: a centrally stored aboveground facility of the Central Organization for Radioactive Waste. This is largely due to transparency. The costs associated with the disposal of nuclear waste are accounted for in today's Dutch consumer electricity prices.

24   Baer, Paul. (2008) *Exploring the 2020 global emissions mitigation gap* (Analysis for the Global Climate Network). Woods Institute for the Environment, Stanford University, Palo Alto, California, 2008; Meinshausen, M. et al., *Greenhouse-gas emission targets for limiting global warming to 2 °C*, Nature 458, 1158-1162, 2009.
        Ranger, N., A. Bowen, J. Lowe, L. Gohar, *Mitigating climate change through reductions in greenhouse gas emissions: the science and economics of future paths for global annual emissions*, December 2009 available at http://www.cccep.ac.uk/Publications/Policy/Policy-docs/bowen-Ranger_MitigatingClimateChange_Dec09.pdf

25   Carbon Dioxide Information Analysis Center, Oak Ridge Labs US, October 2011.

26   Strahan, David, 'The Oil Maze', *New Scientist*, 3 December 2011.

27   *Ibid.*

28   Spinney, Laura, 'The Underhand Ape', *New Scientist*, p. 43, 5 November 2011.

29   *Ibid.*

30   Dawkins, E. et al., Wales' *Ecological Footprint – Scenarios to 2020*, Stockholm Environment Institute for the Welsh Government, 2008.

31   James, Oliver, *Affluenza: How to be Successful and Stay Sane*, Vermilion, 2007.

32   Diamond, Jared, *Collapse: How Societies choose to Fail or Survive*, Penguin, 2006.

33   See Ehrlich, Paul, *The Population Bomb*. Buccaneer, 1968; and Ehrlich. P. and Ehrlich A., *Population Resources and the Environment*, 1970.

34   Kuznets, Simon, *National Income 1929-1932*, 73rd US Congress 2nd Session, 1934.
http://library.bea.gov/us

35   See Daly, H. and Cobb. J., *For the Common Good*. Beacon Boston, 1989: and Nordhaus, W. and Tobin, J. *Is Growth Obsolete*, Columbia University Press, 1972. Professor Peter Midmore, of Aberystwyth University has constructed an ISEW for Wales.

36   Schumacher, E.F., *Small is Beautiful: A Study of Economics as if People really Mattered*, Vintage, 2011 (original edition, 1973).

37   Galbraith, J.K., *The World Economy Since the Wars*, Sinclair-Stevenson, 1994.

38   Hessel, Stephane, *Time for Outrage/Indignez-vous*, Quartet Books, 2011.

39   Hardin, Garrett, 'The Tragedy of the Commons', *Science*, 162, 1243-1249, 1968.

40   Jackson, Tim, *Prosperity Without Growth*, Earthscan, 2011.

41   MacKay, David J.C., *Sustainable Energy – without the hot air*, UIT Cambridge, 2008; available online at www.withouthotair.com

42   Farrar, John. F. et al., *Report on Carbon Footprint to Gwynedd County Council*, 2004.

43   Munday M., Roche N., Christie M., and Midmore P., *Index of Sustainable Economic Welfare for Wales*, Cardiff Business School, 2006; Jackson T., and McBride N., Measuring Progress, Report to European Environmental Agency 2005 and Report to French Government 2010 http://stiglitz-sen-fitoussi.fr/en/index.htm

44   See Kevin Morgan, 'Values for money' in *the welsh agenda*, IWA, Spring 2012.

45   Sandel, Michael. J., *Justice: What's the right thing to do*, Farrar Strauss and Giroux, 2009.

Chapter 11
Scaling Speed
Andy Middleton

It ought to be remembered that there is nothing more difficult to take in hand, more perilous to conduct, or more uncertain in its success, than to take the lead in the introduction of a new order of things. Because the innovator has for enemies all those who have done well under the old conditions, and lukewarm defenders in those who may do well under the new. This coolness arises partly from fear of the opponents, who have the laws on their side, and partly from the incredulity of men, who do not readily believe in new things until they have had a long experience of them.
Niccolò Machiaveli, 1513

And the trouble is, if you don't risk anything, you risk even more.
Erica Jong

With all of its smallness, and a recent history of claims of being in the lead pack on making sustainability work, Wales is at risk of rhetoric becoming reality. We have processes in abundance, yet there's a gap between what we're doing, and what is needed.

If we muster the courage and commitment to bring together our collective imagination and capability into a single, shared narrative, Wales could address climate and biodiversity challenges, build a more resilient economy and provide a beacon of hope to a world wallowing in a sea of incrementalism. Our choice is between this attractive path or another, more familiar and comforting one that would take us back to where we started from last time around.

Stopping for a few minutes is all it takes to start a new journey. Cease travel for long enough to notice where you're standing right now. Look around and scan the horizon. Feel the wind on your face. Smell the earth and rub a handful of its magic in your fingers, holding the sponginess of life to the air. Hear the voices of nature, communities, your neighbours, and ask after their wellbeing. The answers are not what you'll want to be hearing if you were after a quiet and restful night of slumber.

What you see with your eyes and senses set to 'open' won't, of course, be comfortable for anyone who knows what the signs mean. A combination of environmental, social, financial and technological challenges are taking us to the brink of an uncomfortable step that, regardless of direction, will force rapid change. It's change of a type that is paraphrased neatly by Dawn Vance, Director of Global Logistics at Nike:

> "Organisations have three options: (i) hit the wall; (ii) optimise and delay hitting the wall; or (iii), redesign for resilience – simultaneously optimising existing networks whilst embracing disruptive innovation and working collaboratively with partners."

Organisations across Wales and beyond our borders are at risk from being largely unaware, unprepared or both, about the scale of the challenge and the response needed. Equally, there are opportunities for those who prepare effectively, and early.

Before considering alternative directions and options, it's instructive to look back to work out how we got into this mess in the first place. Like many disaster scenarios, a combination of factors conspired to trip us up. For a couple of hundred of years, planners and developers of the current economic model have been using a faulty set of measures that gave incorrect readings of costs and benefits. From the start, we forgot to take account of a major line of expenditure and chose to ignore the cost of the goods and services that we take from nature. The United Nations Environment Programme's Finance Initiative's research showed that:

> "...in 2008, the world's 3,000 largest public companies by market capitalisation were estimated to be causing US$2.15 trillion of environmental damage, equivalent to 7 per cent of their combined revenues and 50 per cent of their combined earnings."[1]

The information around us shows that we are part of nature, and subject to its rules. Taking this into account, communities, organisations and families will have to start paying the full price for the goods and services that they take from nature. The maths are a bit like compound interest. If you continually invest, capital builds and you may be able to live off the interest. Choosing to live on debt, with nature a more powerful judge of balance than any bank, will bring its own painful overdraft experience.

In deciding where we're trying to go with the Welsh Government's Natural Environment Framework and the Sustainability Bill, we should ask the question: what does good enough look like? This is a powerful start point that few use. It's much more comfortable to ask 'what's better?' or 'what's an improvement?' than to explore the uncomfortable uncertainties around 'good enough'. Making things better is comfortable, reassuring and relatively controllable. Making things 'good enough' means stepping into the unknown, crossing boundaries and collaborating with other organisations at a level that's not been seen before.

Conversations with biomimicry specialist Denise DeLuca produced a realisation that nature is set by default to a 'good enough' specification. Homo sapiens appear to be the only species that isn't. The 'R10' framework, illustrated below, uses axes of performance plotted against a focus of effort that ranges from compliance on one side to consciousness on the other to illustrate the difference between incremental improvement and what good enough might be.

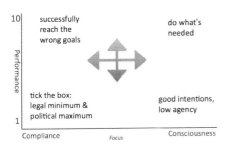 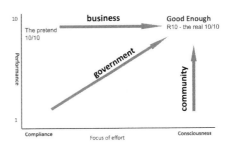

The 'R10' framework

A few of the stark realisations that stem from setting compliance against consciousness in this way include:

1. Most organisations, particularly government, are firmly in the bottom left corner of the R10 frame. A chief executive of a leading Welsh local authority recently responded with a self-score of just 2 out of 10 to the question, "Taking into account everything that's already happening, and what you think is likely, how high would you rate your performance?" His score was framed mostly on compliance.

2. Improving performance by 10 per cent a year results in a doubling time of seven years. That means that a score of 2 today would double to 4 by 2019. Improving poor performance by small margins doesn't address the issues in front of us fast enough.

3. Scoring a 10 out of 10 on the 'compliant' end of the scale still guarantees failure, as the goals were not coded to build resilience in the first place. Ambulance response times based on time not lives saved, or minimising loss of biodiversity rather than restoring it, would be examples of inappropriate targets that are too easily accepted.

4. In the lower right corner in area of good intent, but low agency. This is a space populated by deeply caring, passionate people, often with high levels of skill but relatively narrow skill sets. They may be expert on growing local, organic vegetables, and may not know how to sell them. They may be or wonderful at community engagement but with little knowledge of how to use Twitter or Facebook to communicate in their target audience's preferred medium.

5. In exploring the top right corner, 'R10' describes a 'real 10/10' position, that's good enough, taking into account what we already know. Described through a R10 lens, if successful performance would be copied and scaled widely, and be good for the job ahead of us. If R10 were a bridge, it would cross the river. If it were the Titanic, it would have the same number of lifeboat seats as people on the boat.

R10 is the space where things get interesting, complex, hopeful and full of possibility. Consider this question: "Knowing what you know about existing forthcoming challenges that include mobility, diet, diabetes, food security, debt and community, what percentage of children would you want to be able to cook cheap nutritious food from fresh or dried products by the time that they reached adulthood?" I haven't talked to anyone who has said less than 100 per cent. Prefaced with the same lead in, 'knowing what you already know', the following questions have elicited the same 100 per cent answer:

• What percentage of elected members or government officers would you want to know the fundamental drivers and potential consequences of challenges such as energy and food security, health, debt, public finance, resource scarcity and climate impacts, that are likely to affect the communities that they are elected or paid to represent?

• If you intended to be a leading performer in your sector, what proportion of your staff would be actively engaged in finding potential alternatives to the current business model?

• How many students, on leaving the education process, would have spent time researching and implementing projects, validated by progressive local employers, that could immediately bring value to those that they might work for?

• What percentage of young people, like their employers and representatives in local or national government, would be familiar with the measures and instruments that would be of greatest use when they enter the world of work?

- Of the tens of millions of pounds investment given by local and national government as project or grant funding to businesses and third sector organisations, what proportion would be tied to levels of sustainability performance that were of a 'R10', good enough quality?

One of the first realisations in pondering the 'So, how do we get there?' dilemma is that R10 performance can never be delivered by a single organisation. No council has the resources to teach every young person to cycle or cook; no university has the ability to connect learning to real world outcomes without fully engaging fully with forward-looking employers. R10 outcomes can only be reached when we leave behind the relative security of our short-term focused silos, where ticking the box keeps us safe individually, even if, in winning the battle, we lose the war. The step away from the security of short-term compliance is one that takes us closer to the possibilities of success, where boundaries between organisations change radically and permanently.

To even imagine R10 possibilities requires, for many, a shift in thinking that precedes a shift in outcomes. Typical of the headline indicator moves will be those in the table below:

Past	Future
A focus on developing **leaders**	Nurturing **leadership** throughout entire organisations
Resources invested in creating **long term plans**	Long term **outcomes** determine actions, rather than pre-set plans
Community **engagement** perceived to 'do the job'	**Involvement** in finance, decisions, benefits and choices replaces 'just talk'
Work in **silos** to ensure measurability	Focus on **collaboration** to ensure benefit
Centralise information and decision making	**Localise** ownership, knowledge, responsibility and benefit
Audit 'triple bottom line' outcomes after a project has finished	Use a triple top line **design** approach right from the start
Assume that change is **predictable**	Build in ability to deal with more **surprise**
Ticking the box to prove that the job has been done	**Demonstrating learning** to show that progress has been made

To embark on the first steps towards a more hopeful and resilient future that is capable of meeting humanity's needs for many generations to come, a step change in thinking and practice is needed. The immediate first step is to create the space and time needed to imagine our R10 futures in a way that is far removed from visioning sessions that take little or no account of the current context.

With a clearer understanding of what a radical, 'shock and awesome' view of the future might be, it's possible, by staying in a creative rather than a critical space, to imagine the different relationships that organisations would need to make a shift of this level possible. On the way, we'll need to work carefully and openly with bodies including the Wales Audit Office, the Assembly's Audit and Scrutiny Committees, anti-fraud teams and many others, to design a new canvas onto which new measures of progress might be painted.

Once equipped with a clear sense of what good enough might look like, plus new insights into organisational relationships, it becomes possible to start bridging the gap between now and the future with traditional approaches to problem solving and project management. The difference, though, is that the end point will be somewhere worth reaching, not a waypoint of progress that, although better than the past, is insufficient for the future.

Taking into account the progress, commitments, bills and processes that are already in the system, Wales is in a unique position to join the lead team of countries taking action on sustainability. In doing so, the Welsh Government can send a clear signal to organisations thinking of investing in Wales that we're open for business. That is to say, for those who want to be part of building a successful, resilient and smarter future that is rewarding for the natural infrastructure that supports us as well as for employees, investors and communities. As individuals, by taking a R10 'what's does good enough look like' question into meetings, conferences and planning sessions for the next six months might, just, be enough to start a new conversation.

Notes

1   KPMG, *Expect the Unexpected*, p. 4, 2012.

Notes on contributors

Susan Baker is Professor in Environmental Social Science, at Cardiff University's School of Social Sciences and Lead Academic in the University's Sustainable Places Research Institute. She has a background in political science, economics and philosophy. Her research focuses on the interrelationship between social and ecological processes, with particular emphasis on the problems of global environmental change. Professor Baker was the first woman and social scientist to be awarded the prestigious Royal Appointment to the King of Sweden as King Carl XVI Gustaf Professor in Environmental Science.

Jane Davidson was Minister for Environment and Sustainability in Wales from 2007 to 2011 where she was responsible for the Welsh Government agreeing to make sustainable development its central organising principle. She is now Director of the Institute for Sustainability Practice, Innovation and Resource Effectiveness (INSPIRE) at Trinity Saint David University. She lives on a smallholding in west Wales, is a keen walker, and President of Ramblers Cymru.

Peter Davies was appointed Commissioner for Wales and Vice Chair of the UK Sustainable Development Commission in 2007, providing independent advice to the Welsh and UK Governments. Following the UK Government's abolition of the Commission he was appointed as Wales' first Sustainable Futures Commissioner by Welsh Government in April 2011. This role is supported by Cynnal Cymru – the sustainable development forum for Wales. Peter also was appointed as independent chair of the Climate Change Commission for Wales in 2010.

Katarina Eckerberg is Professor of Political Science at Umeå University in Sweden. She has a professional background in forestry combined with a PhD in political science, and has worked at the Policy and Planning Service of the Food and Agriculture Organisation in Rome and been Deputy Director of the Stockholm Environment Institute as well as serving on a large number of research boards in Sweden, Norway and the EU. She has also been Theme Leader of research on Multilevel Governance of Social-Ecological Systems at the Stockholm Resilience Centre. Her publications include over 100 books and book chapters, journal articles, research reports and popular science articles. She is member of the Editorial Boards of *Environmental Politics, Forest Policy and Economics*, the *Journal of Environmental Policy and Planning and Local Environment*, and has served on several high-level advisory bodies in the field of environment and sustainable development.

Sándor Fülöp was elected to become Hungary's first Parliamentary Commissioner for Future Generations in May 2008. He holds a degree in law from the Eötvös Loránd University of Sciences (1982) and a degree in psychology (1987). Between 1984 and 1991 he worked as a public prosecutor at the Metropolitan and the National Chief Prosecutor's Office. Following a short period of private legal practice at the international law firm Ruttner and Partners (1993-1994) Mr Fülöp acted, until his election as Commissioner, as the director of Hungary's principal non-profit environmental law firm, the Environmental Management and Law Association. During this period he also held a number of international positions. He participated in the drafting of the 1998 UN ECE Convention on Access to Information, Access to Decision-making and Access to Justice in Environmental Matters (the Aarhus Convention). Between 2002 and 2008 he was a member of the Compliance Committee of the Aarhus Convention. Mr Fülöp has been a university lecturer on environmental law since 1997.

Anne Meikle is Head of WWF Cymru. Born in Scotland, she trained as a psychologist and she has worked in the private, public and voluntary sectors. She has been a manager at a multi-national paper company, worked for the Brecon Beacons National Park, and also managed an environmental volunteering charity and its social enterprise arm. As Head of WWF in Wales, she leads the team and represents the organisation in the media. Backed by the policy and communications resources of the Welsh staff and UK organisations, she seeks to influence decision-makers on issues such as marine legislation, sustainable development and climate change.

Andy Middleton is a social entrepreneur, change agent and speaker. He is Founder Director of The TYF Group, the St Davids-based sustainable innovation, education and adventure business, Director of TYF CIC, Director of Enviro Pass Ltd and Associate Director of INSPIRE. He draws on 25 years experience of work and learning in dynamic natural environments to design projects, interventions and workshops that give leaders and managers tools for change. Andy is currently bringing 20 selected corporate, public and third sector organisations to set new 'land speed records' for sustainability and find out how fast it's possible to go when collaboration works alongside competition.

John Osmond is Director of the Institute of Welsh Affairs, and has written widely on Welsh politics, culture, and devolution. His publications include *Crossing the Rubicon: Coalition Politics Welsh Style* (2007); *Birth of Welsh Democracy: the first term of the National Assembly for Wales* (Editor, 2003); and *Welsh Europeans* (1997). A former journalist and television producer he is a Fellow of Cardiff Metropolitan University and has been awarded an Honorary MA by the University of Wales.

Stephen Palmer is Archie Cochrane Professor of Epidemiology and Public Health, at Cardiff University. From 2003-5 he was also director of the Health Protection Agency's Chemical Hazards Division, and from 2006-2009 Director of Local and Regional Services for England, dealing with outbreaks and environmental threats. In 2008 he was awarded the Royal College of Physicians Faculty of Public Health Alwyn Smith Prize for his 'outstanding contribution to the health of the public'. He was a member of the UK government's National Expert Panel on New and Emerging Infections from 2003-2010. More recently he has developed research into the built environment and health and leads the health theme in Cardiff University's Sustainable Places Research Institute.

Anna Nicholl is a freelance policy and research consultant and an Associate of the Institute of Welsh Affairs. She was a Special Adviser to the First Minister and Cabinet in the One Wales coalition government 2007-11. She has worked in various roles in the voluntary sector including as Director of Policy and Communications at the Welsh Refugee Council. She has a particular interest in civil society and was a Commissioner on the Carnegie UK Trust's Inquiry into the Future of Civil Society in the UK and Ireland.

Tim Peppin has been Director of Regeneration and Sustainable Development at the Welsh Local Government Association since December 2007. The portfolio covers a wide range of environmental and regeneration issues including waste (policy, awareness and improvement), transport, planning, regeneration initiatives, economic, business and community development, flood and water, countryside and biodiversity, National Parks, rural regeneration as well as corporate roles in relation to European issues and sustainable development. Tim has worked in a wide range of roles in local government since 1988.

Peter Roderick is a public interest environmental lawyer and a member of the Alliance for Future Generations. He is author of *Taking the Longer View: UK Governance Options for a Finite Planet* (WWF-UK, 2010); *The National Assembly for Wales and Taking the Longer View* (WWF-Cymru, 2011); and the *Draft Declaration on Planetary Boundaries* (WWF-UK, 2011). He has almost thirty years of experience working as a barrister in private practise, in the oil industry and for organisations such as Friends of the Earth and the World Future Council.

Andrea Ross is a Reader in the School of Law at the University of Dundee and author of *Sustainable Development Law in the UK from Rhetoric to Reality* (Earthscan /

Routledge). Among other things, this explores how law can be used to support best practice in implementing sustainable development. An advocate of sustainability literacy in law students she developed some of the UK's first modules in Sustainable Development Law and Environmental Justice which have been replicated elsewhere. She has contributed to inquiries both in the UK and Scottish Parliaments and is the academic member of the Law Society of Scotland's planning law sub-committee.

Gareth Wyn Jones originally trained in biological chemistry. Research work on the mechanisms of plant adaptation to stressful environments led to an interest in rural development, initially in third world countries, and in the interrelationship of agricultural production, environmental constraints and conservation and economic development. He directed the Centre for Arid Zone Studies at Bangor University for a number of years, helping also to manage the Department for International Development's strategic research programme. Later he joined the newly established Countryside Council for Wales as Deputy Chief Executive and Chief Scientist. He has served with a number of international and Welsh organisations including the National Museum, Amlwch Industrial Heritage Trust, National Trust Wales, Wales Rural Forum and the IWA's North Wales Branch. He chairs the Welsh Government's group on 'Land Use and Climate Change'.